Student Ministry and the Supremacy of Christ

Richard Ross

CROSS

BOOKS

CrossBooks™
1663 Liberty Drive
Bloomington, IN 47403
www.crossbooks.com
Phone: 1-866-879-0502

First published by CrossBooks 10/8/2009

ISBN: 978-1-6150-7055-8 (sc)

Library of Congress Control Number: 2009936948

Bible default translation is NASB. Others used are NIV, NKJV and The Message.

Printed in the United States of America
Bloomington, Indiana

This book is printed on acid-free paper.

Supremacy—
Supreme power and authority

Colossians 1:18:
". . . so that in everything he might have the *supremacy*" (NIV).

". . . so that He Himself will come to have first place in everything."

". . . that in all things He may have the preeminence" (NKJV).

Contents

Preface

Some say in five years we will be the same as we are today except for the people we meet and the books we read.

I am not the person I was five years ago. The instruments God has used to make that so are a person I met and a book I read. David Bryant is the person, and *Christ Is All* is the book.

I met David at a New York City airport on November 6, 2006. We had just discovered we were on missions that seemed to mesh. David was (and is) giving his life to foster a hope-filled awakening to the supremacy of Christ in the church at large. I was (and am) on a quest to see Christ worshipped and adored without distractions by students and their parents and leaders. From the moment we met, those missions intertwined beautifully.

Actually, David Bryant had been impacting my life for decades before we actually met. In 1988 David founded Concerts of Prayer International and guided it for the next fifteen years. Participating in concerts of prayer over those years reshaped my prayer life and set me on a quest to discover much more about conversing with Triune God.

On October 4, 1997 I stood on the National Mall in Washington, D.C. with well over one million Christian men. The day was called Stand in the Gap. I could not see the stage, but I could hear a voice early in the day that invited us to fall on our knees, silent in prayer before the King of glory. My time with face against the soil was one of the holiest of my life. In 2006 I discovered that the voice calling us to prayer belonged to David Bryant.

For many years my involvement with the Youth Ministry Executive Council has opened a door to be in Washington, D.C. for the National Day of Prayer. For years my spirit resonated with David Bryant, chairperson of the National Prayer Committee for nine years, as he called Christians throughout America to prayer. I just never guessed I would meet him or walk beside him.

In 2003 David founded Proclaim Hope! Now his life mission is:

1. To proclaim a more comprehensive vision of Christ and His supremacy throughout the Church.

2. To awaken for all believers a life-changing hope focused on this larger vision of Christ and His supremacy.

3. To empower the ministry of Christians and churches by helping them recover and apply this dynamic hope in Christ so as to mobilize God's people to share in new advances of His kingdom.

4. To equip Christian leaders to become "Messengers of Hope" and Christ-proclaimers who are able to replicate with others the same mission: proclaim, awaken, and empower.

Soon after I met David, I became aware of David's seminal book on Christology titled *Christ Is All! A Joyful Manifesto on the Supremacy of God's Son* (available at www.ChristIsAllBook.com). It incorporates three books in one: volume 1 overviews the supremacy of Christ; volume 2 analyzes the "crisis of supremacy" inside the American church; and volume 3 outlines practical strategies for implementing a "Campaign of Hope" anywhere that confronts and cures the crisis within churches and communities.

No book I have read in middle adulthood has had a deeper impact on my life. My first copy is so well used it is held together by rubber bands. The book has become my most common gift to family and friends. Those who read it are not the same.

To the reader of *Student Ministry and the Supremacy of Christ*, I need to say:

1. If any thoughts from this book become part of your own awakening to much more of who the Son is today, you need to know David Bryant is the instrument through whom the Father honed those thoughts.

2. If particular words and phrases especially were helpful in filling you with hope concerning a Christ awakening, you need to know those words likely were David's. He graciously has allowed me to quote his writings at will without frustrating readers with continual quotation marks.

3. If any thoughts from the book you hold create new interest in who Christ is, you must go on to read *Christ Is All*. What this book only can touch on, David develops in depth in his meaty text.

David has defined the core crisis in the Western church. And he has crafted the hope-filled answer to that crisis. All the while, he is too humble to realize his is the most strategic voice for the church in our day. He carries the aroma of the Christ who is the focus of his life and message, and I am honored to call him mentor and friend.

Chapter One
Can You Imagine?

Just for a moment, use your imagination . . .

You arrive at church on Sunday morning. As you pull into your favorite parking spot, you have to sit a moment to reflect. The buildings look about the same, but you have to smile when you think about all the inside changes you have seen in recent days.

The fact that the parking lot is filling faster than usual is evidence of those changes. The faces of children, teenagers, and adults show anticipation for the early worship service. You recall that as church members began to wake up to Christ in all His kingly glory, suddenly adoring Him in worship became a delight. Now they look forward to every service.

Even from the parking lot you can hear the musicians preparing. In recent days the congregation has developed more appreciation for those who lead worship, but the worshippers seem to focus less on them while they sing and offer praise. Instead, you get the distinct impression that worshippers of all ages are lifting their gaze and attention to the Son, sitting enthroned at the right hand of the Father.

Because teenagers are the focus of your life, watching their worship come alive has brought you the greatest joy. When they began to embrace the supreme majesty of Christ, He became the focus of their worship rather than people on the platform. Their worship became as passionate in your church on Sunday morning as in a concert arena on Saturday night.

Sixteen-year-old Samantha pulls into the parking space next to yours, her family laughing as you pretend to panic. Their warmth and laughter as they get out of the car are so different from a year ago. Back then they were hurting one another so often they could hardly wait to

1

separate when they got to church. Now Samantha tells you she feels so close to her dad that she really enjoys the times he gathers the family to pray.

As you enter the lobby, you have to pause in front of the bulletin board that focuses on college students away at school. Investing in teenagers for six years is so rewarding when you see most of them alive for Christ during their college days. You are so thankful the days are over when most of the college students seemed to have lost their faith.

Programs certainly were not enough to sustain them into young adulthood. The change came when teenagers began to wake up to much more of who Jesus Christ is today. This awakening to His supremacy quickly led to adoring Him with a passion the students had not experienced before. You are not surprised that the depth of their love for Him in high school is now reflected in pictures of them leading dorm Bible studies and mission trips to unreached people groups.

As you cross the lobby, you pause to say a kind word to a group of teenagers enjoying conversation. You decide not to interrupt when you hear one of them say, "I'll tell you guys straight up. I think He was more of a mascot than the Monarch of heaven to me. Man, am I glad He didn't leave me there." You pause to wonder if, this time last year, you ever walked up on conversations where teenagers were just talking about Jesus.

As you enter the auditorium, you see ninth-grade Robby in his always-black T-shirt. Just seeing him brings a little sting as you think about all the ways life has been hard for him. But this morning you are encouraged as you see one of the senior adults quickly walking to Robby. Robby can't help but smile when he gets a hug and some warm words from a man who reminds him of his grandfather.

You just shake your head a bit, wondering why anyone thought it was a good idea for teenagers to spend all their time with teenagers— mostly cut off from the rest of the congregation. But you know the church will never go back to that, not with so many adults and teenagers now enjoying relationships and falling more in love with Christ together.

After one more hug, you see Robby walk down near the platform where several students have knelt on the steps to pray for the service.

In some ways it seems the teenagers have led the entire church to make prayer much more than a formality.

As you slide into your favorite pew, an insight comes to you for the first time. The awakening back to Christ in your church spread far more quickly because teenagers and adults had begun to build heart connections with one another. The generations were able to exchange their discoveries about Christ because relationships already were in place. You feel pretty certain this is how church is supposed to be.

As you prepare to sing, you almost can imagine the huge door of the throne room swinging open. With a wonderful mixture of warmth and awe, you begin to approach King Jesus seated on high. Now Sunday after Sunday you approach Him with a depth of adoration you once only tasted during the "Hallelujah Chorus" at Christmas. Today, recent discoveries you made about Christ in Scripture give you fresh ways to honor Him. You already are looking forward to hearing new ways He will invite you to join Him in what He is doing on earth.

You stand to your feet as the music begins. You glance over toward some teenagers who are singing as if they are in the throne room too. The passionate radiance on their faces brings a tear to your eyes. They have profited from your friendship and your creativity and your teaching. But with deep humility you realize that what they most needed from you was your own awakening to the supremacy of God's Son. Now that the awakening is spreading, you know all of you are off on the adventure of a lifetime.

Does this imaginary scene seem almost impossible to you? It isn't. Not with Christ on His throne. The pages that follow will make clear that . . .

- Student ministry begins with a focus on the supremacy of the Son of God.

- Students are most likely to embrace the full extent of the supremacy of Christ when they have heart connections with significant adults in their lives who increasingly embrace the full supremacy of Christ.

✢ • The sovereign Father of the universe has the power to exalt His Son *in your church.*

No matter what discouragements you have experienced in the past, have hope!

For the glory of the Father and by the power of the Spirit,
   an awakening to the supremacy of the Son
     can begin to spread among your students and in your congregation.

Chapter Two
The Crisis in Student Ministry

Christian teenagers know and love Jesus. They really do. But most tend to know Him as a friend and not much more.

Teenagers invited to give a public testimony often say, "I just love Jesus. He's always there for me." By that they may mean Jesus is getting them through hard times at home or with friends. And of course, Jesus *is* very in touch with every life challenge they face, and He *is* omnipotent in His ability to intervene in any situation.

But notice the primary focus of the teenage testimony: "He's always there for *me*." Many believing students tend to know Jesus primarily as a friend who brings *them* good things.

Worst case, some students may see Jesus as their little buddy who rides with them in their shirt pocket. He always is there in case they need to pull Him out to "poof" some difficulty away. But the problem is, students may believe He can be returned to their pocket—conveniently out of sight and out of mind until needed again.

Student ministry is packed with shortcomings. But are there *any* greater than this limited view of Christ?

- Will students who serve a *buddy* ever become bold about their faith?

- Will those who sing to *someone in their shirt pocket* ever become passionate worshippers?

- Will someone who only is the *heavenly Santa* influence decisions on prom night?

- Will those who only know *a little friend* ever rise up to take Him to the nations?

- Will those who love a *youth group mascot* ever bring a spiritual freshening to sleepy churches?

Rick Lawrence observes: "It's clear that despite our best efforts—all our training, commitment, resources, and creativity—today's teenagers are just not getting who Jesus really is, or they're not getting enough of who he really is, or they're getting, literally, a fake Jesus. As a result, few of them are living passionately with Christ in their everyday life. . . . [M]aybe 85 percent of youth-group teenagers aren't getting to know Jesus intimately at church."[1]

The concept of "little Jesus in my pocket" is similar to the term "moral therapeutic deism." This is the term coined by Christian Smith and a team of researchers to describe the faith of America's churchgoing teenagers. The seminal National Study of Youth and Religion found that most American teenagers tend to believe:

1. A God exists who created and orders the world and watches over human life on earth.

2. God wants people to be good, nice, and fair to one another, as taught in the Bible and by most world religions.

3. The central goal of life is to be happy and to feel good about oneself.

4. God does not need to be particularly involved in one's life except when He is needed to resolve a problem.

5. Good people go to heaven when they die.[2]

Where Did Students Get Their Limited View of Christ?

If students today primarily know Jesus as a friend who gives gifts, where do you think they got that idea? Is it possible they have grown up surrounded by Christian adults who also embrace Christ for His benefits, a Christ who is too small?

For good or ill, teenagers closely resemble the spiritual lives of their parents, student ministers, volunteers, and congregations. If most believing teenagers have an inadequate view of Christ, perhaps some of the key adults in their lives also need to be reintroduced to the *real* Jesus for *all* He is.

How Do Many Believers See Christ Today?

Perhaps teenagers and adults have settled for sleepy, sentimental, scaled-down versions of the One who reigns supreme. Perhaps they seldom see Christ as Lord over creation, over history, over the church, and over all the ages to come. Perhaps seldom do their hearts and minds get intrigued with *Him* above everything else.

Perhaps some have redefined the Lord Jesus Christ as:

- *A Handyman*—seen as a source of quick fixes, to deal with adversities by providing instant solutions on command.

- *An Interior Decorator*—contracted to enhance church activities, giving them that extra something.

- *An Emergency Medical Technician*—ready to be brought in quickly at those points where believers finally have exhausted their own ingenuity and resources.

- *A Personal Trainer*—kept on retainer, the way one depends on a golf coach, to provide practical pointers in order to play the game of life a little more successfully.

- *A Pharmacist*—dispensing self-discoveries, putting healing balm on hurting hearts, or prescribing pills for the suffering life throws at Christians.

Each of these limited views of Christ holds an element of truth, to be sure. He *is* available for emergencies. He *can* transform everything believers do for the Father into something beautiful. Of course He trains, cures, and inspires. Yet each of these, when taken alone, reveals too little hope in Christ's glorious greatness.

Have Many Believers Made Christ Their Mascot?

Knowing Christ as a *mascot* may be the most descriptive (and most disturbing) of all the self-serving visions of the Lord. Believers welcome

Him to cheer them on, to inspire their efforts, to give them confidence about the outcome of the contest. They're so proud of Him! So happy to be identified with His name. Enthusiasm for Him energizes Christians—for a while.

But with Christ as a mascot, the "game" is really about *believers*, not about Him. They call the plays, organize the team, execute the strategies, pile up the points, and achieve the wins. Most of the time Jesus is relegated to the sidelines as their figurehead—the "name" by which they take the field, the definition of all they aspire to, the one they call on when they get behind. The cheers may be for Him, but their victories are for themselves.

As contradictory as it may seem, many have redefined Jesus into someone they can both admire *and* ignore at the same time! To be their *mascot*, they've redesigned Him to be reasonably convenient—someone praiseworthy, to be sure, but overall kept in reserve, useful, "on call" as required.

Missing is the fact that God enthroned His Son at His right hand and that Christ is reigning over all things. Without promoting an overriding passion for Christ as Monarch—as *everything*—why would believers ever openly celebrate Him as anything other than their mascot?

Rarely does it cross the minds of some that the *supremacy* of Christ means He *is* the game. He coaches the players, calls the strategies, quarterbacks the plays, achieves the touchdowns, wins the game, and gets the "write up" next day. The team has no existence, and no reason to exist, apart from Him. From Him, through Him, for Him, under Him, in Him, and to Him are all things. And every fan in the stands must bow at His feet before they dare to cheer in His name.

Is This Limited View of Christ a Crisis?

Where Christ reigns there is hope. Always. When the church embraces the full supremacy of the Son of God, there is passion. Always. Hope is draining from the Western church. In most places, passion is about gone. The anemia of most student ministries and most churches *proves* there is a crisis in Christology.

John said: "Anyone who runs ahead and does not continue in the teaching about Christ does not have God" (2 John 9 NIV). No exceptions! Could anything be more debilitating for the global cause of Christ than this verdict? Even *Christians* can come up short on how they view and value the *supremacy* of God's Son.

This shortfall has blindsided far too many believers. It has drained the vitality from worship, prayer, community life, and ministry outreach. In too many cases it has numbed many believers' daily walk with their Redeemer. Above all, it has robbed God of His rightful praise through His people among all peoples.

How regularly do teenagers and adults worship Christ as their:

- *Sovereign Son of the Father*, reigning at His right hand forever and ever?

- *Triumphant Victor* over sin, death, and Hades?

- *Glorious Conqueror*, the dominating personality for all ages to come?

- *Unequivocal Commander* of heaven's hosts, ready to obey His every word?

- *Indisputable Judge* of peoples and nations, to whom all must give an account?

- *Undeniable Ruler* of history, overseeing its path and its outcome from beginning to end?

- *Incomparable King* of an Empire who ultimately will fill creation with His power and piety?

- *Irreplaceable Head and Heart* of a people whom He has bought with His own blood?

- *Reigning Redeemer* of the church universal, militant and triumphant?

- *Supreme Lord* in this moment just as fully as He will be Supreme Lord at the end of time?

The Disappearing Names of Christ

The broader church almost has stopped speaking of Christ in such terms. Need proof?

1. Take from your shelves three or four Christian nonfiction best sellers. Quickly scan the pages, looking for names of Christ. You may find a few references to what Christ said or did during His incarnation, but try to find references to who He is *today*. Even if the book you are checking sold millions of copies, you likely will find few or none.

2. Then go to blogs to see what Christian leaders are discussing. Notice how long you will search before finding even one thread dealing with the supremacy of Christ.

3. Examine podcasts from some of the most famous preachers and speakers in the land. They may use the generic "God" scores of times in a sermon, but do they make specific reference to Christ (other than quoting Him from His time on earth)?

4. Scan your own computer for talks you have given and lessons you have composed. Have you been speaking about the reign and majesty of God's Son? Have you also used generic "God" almost exclusively? When was your most recent talk that left students more in awe of the present glory of the Son?

Would you say it is a crisis that the church Christ founded has just about stopped calling Him by name?

How Do Those around You See Christ?

Monitor conversations among Christian teenagers and adults. Listen as well to what you hear taught in classes and groups. Ask yourself two questions:

1. How often do I hear the name of the Lord Jesus mentioned *at all* (apart from quoting one of His sayings or referring to His life on earth)?

2. Whenever I hear His name, if I do, are the things said about Him intended in any way to magnify more clearly His glory as God's Son?

In other words, do the Christian teenagers and adults around you ever spend time talking to one another about the *supremacy* of God's Son (by whatever terms they use)?

How about You?

Do you tend to believe Christ only exists to bless you and to give you the kind of life *you* want? Do you primarily expect from Him relief from suffering, quick solutions to your problems, and general satisfaction with life? Have you assumed He is the key to "the American dream" of becoming increasingly prosperous and stress free? If the students closest to you see Jesus as a little friend with benefits, is it possible they picked this up from you? Ask yourself . . .

1. Who really is the Christ through whom you were converted in the first place? Even more importantly, do you sense He truly *conquered* your heart that day, the way a King of kings has every right to do?

2. Do you sense as reigning Lord He *still* maintains full sway over you right now?

3. Are you *convinced* all the promises of God are really and truly summed up in His Son? Or do you still struggle with hopelessness? Do you view God's promises as *totally available* to you in Christ Jesus?

4. Do you expect Him to back His claims that He will ultimately be victorious over every challenge you confront? If so, how do you exhibit such convictions? What kinds of

practical differences does this make in your daily walk with Him?

In short, are you captivated by Christ as His Royal Highness? Or for all practical purposes has He evolved in your thinking to a figurehead? Observing your daily walk with Him, what would fellow believers conclude? Which model of the Lord's role, Monarch or mascot, would they find at work in your life?

But what if you begin to wake up to more and more of who Christ is today? And what if you begin to wake up other teenagers, parents, volunteers, and members of the congregation?

What if increasing numbers of believers begin to declare: "May all *Christians* confess—and ultimately *proclaim*—Jesus Christ as Lord, the *supreme* Lord of His church!"

Then something wonderful may happen! A reawakening of fresh hope and passion toward Christ may be released in His body. Believers will once again know Him not only as Lord over global concerns but as the One who is *their* "all in all," as the One supreme over *them* forever.

Are you ready to say . . .

- In light of all Christ is, there is far *more* of Him to know than I've yet discovered.

- Therefore, I must be passionate to know Him much more than I am.

- And I must draw near to Him with far more hope in Him than ever before.

- God longs for the church to discover much more about His Son.

- I must, therefore, proclaim Him to believers more fully than ever.

- I must never fear praying or proclaiming His glory too much.

Chapter Three
The Supremacy of Christ

To be blunt, many Christians need to meet God's Son again. As they do, it may feel as if it were happening for the first time because of how far from His glory many have wandered.

How Would *You* Define a Biblical Vision of the Supremacy of Christ?

The Father is so thoroughly consumed with the primacy of His Son that He insists on being known as "the Father of our Lord Jesus Christ." Can believers choose to be any less passionate about this same Person? Should believers not be inspired by how the Father exalts His Son?

Two weeks ago I stood in DFW Airport to welcome home my only son Clayton. He had spent six weeks backpacking the good news into remote regions of Ethiopia. As I saw him coming up the concourse, my heart was full of joy because of his faithfulness to his call even though sacrifice was involved. And right then a thought swept over me that brought tears to my eyes. It dawned on me that God the Father also stood in the concourses of heaven, watching for His Son to return from His mission. Forty days after the resurrection, the ascended Son walked back into heaven. I tried to multiply what I was feeling in the airport times a quadrillion, imagining the delight of a Father over a Son who at great sacrifice had just won the redemption of all humankind. Is it any wonder the beaming Father enthroned His Son at His right hand and placed in His hand the scepter of all authority?

Colossians 1:18 reports that for God the bottom line of every constellation He's created—the stunning climax of every facet of salvation He offers—comes down to this: *"that in everything [Christ] might have the supremacy"* (NIV).

Martin Luther noted, "For nothing counts with God, except His beloved Son, Jesus Christ, who is completely pure and holy before Him. Where He is, there God looks and has his pleasure."[1]

If securing Christ's reputation is such a big deal to heaven, should it not be equally a big deal for all of heaven's citizens? Should believers not eagerly join with the Spirit in His role to promote Christ's preeminence in all things?

Jesus explained it this way: "He (the Spirit) will glorify Me, for He will take of Mine and will disclose it to you. All things that the Father has are Mine; therefore I said that He takes of Mine and will disclose it to you" (John 16:14–15).

Teenagers and adults need to revisit the one word Paul uses to gather up the whole panorama of Christ's glory: *supremacy.*

How Does the *Supremacy* of Christ Take Us beyond the *Centrality* of Christ?

When describing the *supremacy* (supreme power and authority) of God's Son, Scripture points toward much more than what Christians commonly refer to as His *centrality*. Of course, centrality remains an important biblical concept. It characterizes a whole set of Jesus' lordship claims. It affirms Him as the center of everything, meant to be in the middle of everything, surrounded by everything. And, *that* He is!

But supremacy takes a vision of Him to a whole new level. Similar to centrality, His claims to supremacy rise from His nature as God's Son. But this dimension gives the Redeemer even higher homage. As supreme, the Lord is not only surrounded by everything, but He must also *surround* everything with Himself. As Lord, He *encompasses* all within His rule.

Of course, Christians properly profess that "Jesus is the center of my life." And that is true! But *which* Jesus is at the center of my life?—that is the issue. Is it the one whose glory *enfolds* my life, *consumes* my life, and *defines* my life because He alone thoroughly *sums up* my life in Himself? Or just the little Jesus who rides in my pocket?

On one hand centrality calls believers to let their lives be *wrapped around* who Jesus is. On the other hand, supremacy requires that their lives also be *wrapped up into* who Jesus is. Without question there is a delightful difference between these two complementary positions.

Centrality is about Christ's right to be kept at the center of who *we* are, where *we* are headed, all *we* are doing, and how *we* are blessed.

Supremacy speaks of so much more.
It proclaims Christ's right to keep us at the center of
who *He* is, where *He* is headed,
what *He* is imparting, and how *He* is blessed.

Who Do *You* Say He Is?

Remember the debate the twelve had about Jesus as they walked the roads of Caesarea Phillipi? They were responding to Jesus' penetrating question to Peter: *"Who do you say that I am?"* (Matt. 16:15). Finally, Peter answered with the familiar words, "You are the Christ, the Son of the living God" (v. 16).

In another place, the Lord Jesus answered His own question to Peter when He said to John: "I am the Alpha and the Omega, the first and the last, the beginning and the end" (Rev. 22:13). Not only was He at the beginning, but He Himself *is* the beginning. Not only will He be waiting for believers at the end, He *is* the end.

All history streams from Him and is directed toward Him, to be completed by Him. The eternal past has no other eternal future but Christ alone. There is only *One* in the entire universe of whom God has ever said without qualification: "In You I am well-pleased" (Luke 3:22). Thus Christ and Christ alone can insist on being the One to whom all supremacy (supreme power and authority) belongs, whose supremacy encompasses all.

Do you believe Christ will be more glorious than we can imagine on the day of His return? Do you think believers will be wonderfully overwhelmed when they see Him split open the heavens and descend to earth? Absorb this thought: Who Christ will be that day is precisely who He is today. Precisely. In your prayer time this morning, is that how you saw Him in your mind's eye? Did your awe of Him cause you to spend more time praising and adoring Him than making requests of Him?

Dietrich Bonhoeffer wrote, "In Jesus Christ the reality of God entered into the reality of this world. . . . Henceforth one can speak neither of God nor of the world without speaking of Jesus Christ. All concepts of reality which do not take account of Him are abstractions."[2]

The implications of this outlook are extraordinarily life giving.

- This vision enlarges the content of worship.

- It empowers moral perseverance within a decadent culture.

- It inspires renewed efforts at racial reconciliation, at reaching and serving the poor, at rearing godly children, at setting biblical priorities in spending, at performing with excellence on the job, or at spreading the gospel among the nations.

- It fills believers with abounding hope in God even in the darkest moments of the daily battle believers all face.

Where Does the Trinity Fit into Hope in Christ?

Confessing Christ as supreme does not suggest that Jesus is all there is to God, that all deity has been collapsed into Christ alone, that believers' destiny is *only* about Him. Maintaining the supremacy of the Lord Jesus Christ for all eternity will never cease to be a *trinitarian* project. Every dimension of hope is initiated by the Father, developed by the Spirit, while always exalting the Son. The radiance Christ brings us, as the Son of the Father, is inseparable from the fundamental nature of the Godhead—just as the rays of the physical sun could never exist apart from the sun itself.

Even at the end of time, the mission of the Son will be to secure before the whole universe the glory *of* the Godhead *for* the Godhead. One day this will come about fully as He submits Himself (and everything He has conquered), by the Spirit, to the Father's pleasure. Yet even that will only happen once the Father, by the Spirit, has secured for His Son the full recognition of His lordship over everything "in heaven and on earth and under the earth" (Phil. 2:10; compare Phil. 2:5–11 with 1 Cor. 15:20–28 and Rev. 5).

The Son will prevail steadfastly at the center of the Father's throne, world without end, while the Spirit's fires illuminate Him there, for elders and angels (and all of us) to behold and adore with abandon (Rev. 4–5, 21). Permission to live for Him with passion at this moment springs from the passion that will be required of believers when His glory is fully revealed.

Will You Call Believers to Hope in Christ?

Why is *hope* so often a chief hallmark of a life or student ministry where Christ is worshipped as "all in all"? It is because biblical hope is more than a verb (as in "I hope so"). Biblical hope is ultimately a *person* (as in "my hope is in the Lord").

> To revitalize the whole church to take the whole gospel to the whole world, we must restore the *whole vision* of God's Son among God's people.

> We must proclaim a message that "reconverts" Christians back to Christ for *all* He is, for the completion of the Great Commission and the consummation of the ages.

God knows hope is infectious. It spreads life to life, from Christ to you; then from you to students, parents, and volunteers. Where people gather around His Son, hope explodes so that they hold to a vision of His supremacy, living and serving with their eyes on the End Himself. Believers need one another, to *inspire* and *refire* one another, to stir up faith and confidence toward God, to purify passion for Christ and His global cause, and to remain fully alive to all the hope believers were meant to have.

After you stand before God's people—whatever the audience's makeup, size, or agenda—whatever a meeting's immediate text, topic, or concern may be—always ask:

Did they encounter
a larger vision of Christ and His supremacy,
and were they gripped by stronger reasons
to put their hope more fully in Him
than they had before we came together?

Would you like to become a Christ proclaimer to God's people? Would you like to move forward with God's Spirit in a student ministry that changes strategically a movement for the next generation? If so, spread the word!

Lord Jesus . . .

- *You are the Superlative One.* No language is adequate to describe You. No analysis can fully record all the roles You must play to advance God's ever-expanding kingdom (1 Pet. 1).

- *You are the Incomparable One.* Your importance will continue to eclipse all others, outranking every other being in heaven, on earth, or in hell. You will reign "world without end" (Eph. 3:21 KJV).

- *You are the Exalted One.* For eternity You will forever hold the primary focus of our praises, a position of unrivaled distinction, prestige, and majesty in the universe (Rev. 5).

- *You are the Preeminent One.* As You held the primacy at the beginning ("firstborn of creation," Col. 1:15), so You will at the end ("firstborn from among the dead," v. 18). All things to come are Your possessions, to do with as Your Father pleases.

- *You are the Sufficient One.* You will forever prove totally adequate for all our longings, fears, needs, or heart cries. You are the final inheritance of each of God's children (Phil. 3).

- *You are the Triumphant One.* You will defeat all foes unconditionally—both human and demonic—to emerge forever unthreatened, unhindered, and victorious over all opposition, permanently and forever (Rev. 17).

- *You are the Unifying One.* Bringing all things under Your feet as Lord, You will permanently redeem and reconcile to the Godhead innumerable sinners from all the ages and all the nations. In the consummation, all creation, as well as the church itself, will be held together in perfect harmony by Your irrevocable decrees and Your indestructible might (Heb. 1).

Chapter Four
Students and Awakenings

Is an awakening to Christ possible in your church and student ministry? Absolutely. That is exactly what the Father has been orchestrating among believers down through the centuries and today.

Awakening is a church saturated with the supremacy of Christ by the Spirit of Christ. God floods His church with fresh hope, passion, prayer, and mission by refocusing believers on Christ for all He really is. The awakening then spills into the community and cannot be stopped.

All true awakening is about God's bringing glory to His Son by the power of the Holy Spirit through His church. Between His ascension and His consummation, this is one of the most strategic activities of the Holy Spirit. Corporate awakening necessitates trinitarian activity: Father initiated, Spirit driven, and Son centered. If any spiritual experience—whether called revival, awakening, or something else—diminishes, bypasses, or leads people away from Christ, it is not of God and holds no hope for any generation.

One could almost say an awakening is like a coronation.

- It leads believers to reaffirm their wholehearted devotion to the Lamb who sits on the throne.

- It reconnects them to His marching orders as their King.

- It serves as a powerful sign of the supremacy of Christ.

The renewing reality of awakening should be basically defined as this: Jesus expressing Himself more fully to His people as Lord.

Some use the term *revival* to describe an extraordinary movement of the Holy Spirit producing extraordinary results. God begins, at His choosing and timing, to break the hearts of those seeking Him. There is a profound sense of repentance and focus on the holiness of God. Believers confess these sins openly, restore relationships with Christ and others, and the church is revived. This is different from revivalism, which is entirely human in origin.

Some reserve the term *spiritual awakening* to refer to a time when God transforms not only the church but also whole cultures and continents. Revivals alter the lives of individuals; awakenings alter the worldview of a whole people or culture.

In an awakening to Christ, God accelerates, intensifies, deepens, and extends the newness His Son secured for believers by His cross and resurrection. At the same time believers' capacity to express this newness and to minister it to others increases.

If awakening itself becomes their goal, believers may never see it. Awakening must never become an end in itself but a means to an even higher end, the glory of Christ Jesus being revealed and His kingdom coming on earth.

If the church is blind to its true spiritual condition, then awakening simply will be viewed as a divine additive, given basically to increase the effectiveness of ministries. The longing of the heart and the focus of prayers is not awakening; it is Jesus.

Awakening is one of the most exciting expressions of Christ's supremacy any believer can experience until He comes again. When He does, believers will enter into an awakening of such unparalleled proportions that all the other awakenings will become, by comparison, like the faded memories of childhood adventures.

The Pressing Need for Revival and Awakening

The need could not be greater for the revival of God's people today.

- A deficient vision for Christ's glory plagues today's church.

- A desperate loss of hope in Christ's glory exhausts today's church.

- A pervasive loss of passion toward Christ's glory weakens today's church.

- A diminished worship of Christ's glory impoverishes today's church.

Students and Awakening

Down through the centuries God often has allowed students to be the kindling for the fires of revival. Alvin Reid is a student of such revivals. He notes some of the reasons sovereign God might turn to students when He is ready to awaken the lethargic church:

- Students are optimistic about God's ability to impact the future.

- Students are keenly aware of the culture's hypocrisy and moral conflicts.

- Students see through the superficiality of God's people.

- Students are easily energized and mobilized for action.

- Students are willing to take risks.

- Students can be courageous and will stand alone against the status quo.

- Students are passionate about a cause that captures their imagination.

During seasons when students have been at the forefront of awakening movements, their lives have been marked by brokenness for sin and radical obedience. They have been bold in sharing their faith and often have witnessed a remarkable harvest of new believers. Multitudes of students awakened to Christ have entered vocational ministry and have become some of the key leaders in the church.

Here are just a few examples of the role of teenagers in awakening.

Josiah

Under King Manasseh, Judah had descended to its lowest depths. He restored the pagan altars, groves, shrines, poles, and stones. He transformed the house of God into a temple for paganism. He sacrificed his own son to Moloch and was addicted to sorcery, witchcraft, and magic. He aggressively promoted the worship of Baal and Asherah, surpassing the cultic practices of the surrounding, heathen nations.

Amon, son of Manasseh, became king and led in the same directions. He vigorously promoted cultic practices. He ruled for only two years. By the end of those two years, Judah was saturated with idolatry.

Josiah, son of Amon, became king of Judah at age eight. At age sixteen, Josiah had a deep experience with God. By age twenty, he had launched religious reform. He systematically abolished idolatry and destroyed the altars to Baal. He destroyed the Asherah obelisks and removed all the vessels used in cultic worship and leveled the groves. He abolished child sacrifices to Moloch and deposed the non-Levitical priests. He reclaimed and sanctified the temple for God.

Josiah led the people in the ratification of the covenant. He restored the observance of the Passover. He restored the Levitical priesthood. Josiah's return of the ark of the covenant led to joyful worship of God. A teenager was the instrument God used to launch the most pervasive awakening among His people in the Old Testament.

The First Great Awakening

During the Great Awakening of 1740, Jonathan Edwards wrote: "The state of the present revival of religion has an awful aspect upon those that are advanced in years. The work has been chiefly amongst the young; and comparatively but few others have been made partakers of it. And indeed it has commonly been so, when God has begun any great work for the revival of his church; he has taken the young people, and has cast off the old and stiff-necked generation."[1]

Second Great Awakening

The first college revival came to Hampton-Sydney in Virginia in 1787. Four students new to the faith began meeting secretly. When discovered, a near riot broke out. The college president, himself converted in the First Great Awakening, reprimanded the persecutors and invited the four to meet in his parlor for prayer. Awakening soon followed, affecting over half the student body.

Over the years an awakening to Christ spread from Hampton-Sydney to other colleges in the East. By the time Yale received a new president in 1795, the spiritual condition was deplorable. Drunkenness, intemperance, profanity, gambling, and licentiousness were common. The new president (grandson of Jonathan Edwards) began to preach truth in chapel, but results were slow in coming. Seven years later two seniors publicly professed their faith in Christ. Soon dozens were powerfully awakened. Half the seniors entered the ministry. Wow

One researcher has cataloged twenty-five revivals during this era. Of those, twenty emphasized the role of youth in the movements.

More than twenty New England ministers distributed a circular letter calling believers to pray for a general awakening. All the major denominations supported this call to prayer. The awakening began to grow and become "great" after this movement of prayer.

The Student Missions Movement

Williams College in Massachusetts had been the scene of discouraging anti-Christian demonstrations, and the new converts formed a secret society. One summer afternoon in 1806, five students met in a maple grove for private prayer, but a sudden thundershower drove them to shelter under a haystack.

There they prayed about a plan to reach the unevangelized world with the message of Christ. As the sun broke through the clouds, one of their number, Samuel J. Mills, gave a decisive word, "We can do it if we will." As a result, their burden increased with their numbers.

Four years later at Andover Theological Seminary, they proposed to ministers of their denomination that several of them be sent overseas as missionaries. After much debate, they decided to form the American Board of Commissioners for Foreign Missions, the first American mission society, soon to be followed by societies in denomination after denomination. Soon missionary enterprises were targeting the nations.

In the 1880s, teams of students began to travel from university to university, calling out students to missions who were caught up in the awakening. By 1887, more than three thousand had made commitments to go overseas.

The students created a new organization, the Student Volunteer Movement for Foreign Missions. Students and adult preachers began touring the universities of many other countries, calling those students to missions as well. The Student Volunteers used the watchword: "The evangelization of the world in this generation." In half a century more than twenty thousand students reached the foreign mission fields.

The Welsh Awakening and Global Awakening

Joseph Jenkins, a pastor in New Quay, Cardiganshire in Wales, began a Young People's Meeting to battle growing worldliness. In a meeting of that group, Jenkins asked, "What does Jesus mean to you?" Poor, shy, teenage Florrie Evans answered, "If no one else will, then I must say that I do love the Lord Jesus Christ with all my heart." This testimony launched a visible manifestation of the Spirit breaking out in the congregation and eventually in many nations around the world.

Florrie and the awakened young people of Jenkins's congregation held missions in other churches in the region to share what had happened to them. The impact was such that the Cardiganshire revival came to the attention of the national press. Further conventions and prayer meetings fueled the awakening up to the time the great preacher Evan Roberts launched his public ministry in September 1904.

February 12, 1905 was declared a Universal Day of Prayer for Students by the World Student Christian Federation. Scores of colleges joined in the call to pray.

One unnamed observer of the Global Awakening observed: "Hundreds of our young men and women had been brought up religiously in the home and the church; but their religion was cold, formal, following routine. . . . Behold the difference! Now our young people flock to the services, prayers flow spontaneously from their lips like water from the spring, praise ascends to heaven like the carol of birds in spring."

Awakening and the Nations

Students swept up in awakening quickly turn their attention to those who do not know Christ. Most begin to share with friends and family close by. Some are mobilized to carry the gospel far away. Some receive a call to make missions their life work. Others receive a call to earn their living by secular means but to be on mission all of their lives. At times God has ordained that awakening launch major movements to carry the gospel to the nations.

Second Great Awakening—The first great wave of students propelled out by awakening carried the gospel to the edges of the continents in the early 1800s.

The Global Awakening—The second great wave of students carried the gospel to the interiors of the continents in the early 1900s.

The Third Great Wave—If God should choose to send awakening in this day, He may call out and launch a third great wave to exalt His Son before the nations. Perhaps He will raise them up to carry the good news to the last unreached people groups on earth.

Raising the Sails for Revival

Awakening comes from God alone. No human-designed formula can compel God to grant it. The church cannot plan it, stage it, or organize it. It may be church obtained, but it is Christ attained. This is the distinguishing mark between revival and human-produced "revivalism."

However, the Holy Spirit—the primary agent of revival—often chooses to work in grace through believers' prayers, Bible studies, worship, fellowship, and daily obedience. Christians can do nothing to guarantee revival at any particular moment, but believers can always intensify preparations for the wonderful gift of God, in keeping with their hope in His promises. Scripture connects God's sovereignty with cooperation in this way: "Consecrate yourselves, for tomorrow the LORD will do wonders among you" (Josh. 3:5). Or as Jesus said: "The time is fulfilled, and the kingdom of God is at hand; repent and believe in the gospel" (Mark 1:15).

To intensify preparations:

Perceive—Spiritual awakening comes as God's Spirit awakens believers to acknowledge not only that revival is urgently needed but also that the promise of revival is for them.

Prioritize—Be willing to say: "A primary hope for my generation is a Christ awakening, beginning in the church. Therefore, out of my commitment to the preeminence of my Lord Jesus, I will give revival high priority in all I do for Him."

Purify—In every revival repentance must have precedence. Everything that disobeys the Holy Spirit—everything that is incompatible with Christ Himself, who is the focus of revival—must be confessed to the Father and put away.

Proclaim—Since "faith comes by hearing," any biblical revival must be a Word-anchored revival. Therefore, Christians should promote the biblical promises for personal and corporate revival, of which there are hundreds. They also should give reports of what God has done and is doing in revival around the world. And Christians should help one another envision what a revival in this generation might look like inside and outside the church.

Prepare—Though biblical revival is preeminently a corporate experience, each believer must be willing and ready to become the starting point for a fresh work of God in His church. Believers should act as if they truly expect God to grant them this gracious work of His Spirit. They should let their efforts at discipleship equip and prepare them for greater manifestations of Christ and His power in them and through them.

Partner—The hope of promised revival requires a new era of spiritual cooperation—among pastors, leaders of prayer movements, denominational leaders, and others—as they stand together to seek and to receive a God-given Christ awakening for their generation and then as they serve it together for His maximum glory in their nation and beyond.

Are you prepared to begin going to bed every night with this thought on your mind?

I know this day
my life has counted strategically for Christ and His kingdom,
promoting His supremacy in the church and among the nations,
for my generation as well as for the generations to come.

Prayer for Awakening

Throughout history concerted prayer movements have provided launching pads for major advances of Christ's kingdom. This was certainly true with the major religious awakenings in this nation the past two centuries. As God's people kept praying, each awakening overflowed into revitalized churches and denominations, significant social reforms, widespread evangelistic ingatherings, and the creation of scores of new mission-sending societies. Today the scope and urgency of prayers going up from literally millions of saints in many nations is a similar awakening to the glory of God's Son. The historical pattern should forewarn us: Get ready! Extraordinary new displays of Christ's dominion are on their way!

Closing

The American church shares many parallels with the first-century church in Laodicea. Christ's words to that church, recorded in Revelation 3:15–21, are vital.

> "I know your deeds, that you are neither cold nor hot; I wish that you were cold or hot. So because you are lukewarm, and neither hot nor cold, I will spit you out of My mouth. Because you say, 'I am rich, and have become wealthy, and have need of nothing,' and you do not know that you are wretched and miserable and poor and blind and naked, I advise you to buy from Me gold refined by fire so that you may become rich, and white garments so that you may clothe yourself, and that the shame of your nakedness will not be revealed; and eye salve to anoint your eyes so that you may see. Those whom I love, I reprove and discipline; therefore be zealous and repent. Behold, I stand at the door and knock; if anyone hears My voice and opens the door, I will come in to him and will dine with him,

and he with Me. He who overcomes, I will grant to him to sit down with Me on My throne, as I also overcame and sat down with My Father on His throne."

- The Laodicean church, as with many churches today, was prosperous, comfortable, and lukewarm.

- The pronouncement of Christ's judgment was awful.

- Christ called believers to embrace Him and his riches, to clothe themselves in His righteousness, and to apply the truth of Scripture to their spiritual vision.

- He promised (and promises) churches that overcome their lethargic condition (by His power) to dine with Him and to sit with Him on his throne.

The choice could not be clearer: believers who nauseate Christ or believers who receive the most remarkable gifts promised to any of the seven churches in Revelation—the best spiritual food and the privilege of reigning with the King of kings. Once believers recognize how far they have fallen, then they will "humble themselves and pray and seek [His] face and turn from their wicked ways" (2 Chron. 7:14).

The road to awakening is paved with contrite and broken hearts. With such a people God is pleased to dwell (Isa. 57:15). Thankfully, Christ is more than willing to transform believers, taking them into a deeper encounter with all He is as Savior and Lord.

Christ is prepared to awaken believers to much more of who He truly is today. Parents and other adults may have the privilege of awakening students to the King. Or the God who is always full of surprises might first ignite students to bring awakening to the church. Either way, the likely outcome will be students who, for the glory of the Father and in the power of the Spirit, spend a lifetime embracing the full supremacy of the Son.

Chapter Five
A New Paradigm for Student Ministry

Leaders with a true kingdom focus cannot be satisfied with how students seem to be doing right after graduation. What if the passion for their faith proves temporary? What if 50 to 70 percent of those who were active in the church youth group cannot be found in church a year later? Would anyone accept that as evidence of effectiveness in student ministry? Student ministry that does not matter for a lifetime does not matter much.

The following statement by David Kinnaman is profoundly important:

Much of the ministry to teenagers in America needs an overhaul—not because churches fail to attract significant numbers of young people, but because so much of those efforts are not creating a sustainable faith beyond high school. There are certainly effective youth ministries across the country, but the levels of disengagement among twentysomethings suggest that youth ministry fails too often at discipleship and faith formation. A new standard for viable youth ministry should be—not the number of attenders, the sophistication of the events, or the "cool" factor of the youth group—but whether teens have the commitment, passion and resources to pursue Christ intentionally and whole-heartedly after they leave the youth ministry nest.[1]

A Goal for Student Ministry

At its root the Christian faith is a relationship. It is a relationship initiated by God who loved individuals so much He sent His Son to redeem them. Triune God draws them into a relationship with Himself for fellowship and adoration, to join Him in His kingdom purposes, and for the display of His splendor. He desires the exaltation of His Son for eternity, not for eighteen years. A goal for student ministry might look like this:

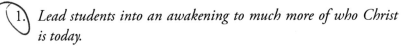

Students who, for the glory of the Father and in the power of the Spirit,
spend a lifetime
embracing the full supremacy of the Son,
responding to His majesty in all of life,
inviting Christ to live His life through them,
and joining Him in making disciples among all peoples.

To move students toward this goal, student ministers:

1. *Lead students into an awakening to much more of who Christ is today.*

   "And Jesus . . . [said], 'All authority has been given to Me in heaven and on earth'" (Matt. 28:18).

   "And [the Son] is the radiance of [God's] glory and the exact representation of His nature, and upholds all things by the word of His power" (Heb. 1:3).

2. *Lead students who increasingly embrace the supremacy (supreme power and authority) of Christ to worship and adore Him more deeply.*

   "Worthy is the Lamb that was slain to receive power and riches and wisdom and might and honor and glory and blessing" (Rev. 5:12).

3. *Lead students enthralled with the wonder of the King to respond to His majesty and lordship in all of life.*

   "Therefore let all the house of Israel know for certain that God has made Him both Lord and Christ" (Acts 2:36).

4. *Lead students to relate to the Son the way the Son relates to the Father.*

"In that day you will know that I am in My Father, and you in Me, and I in you. . . . If anyone loves Me, he will keep My word; and My Father will love him, and We will come to him and make Our abode with him" (John 14:20, 23).

 5. *Lead students to invite Christ to live out His life through them.*

"Christ in you, the hope of glory" (Col. 1:27).

"I have been crucified with Christ; and it is no longer I who live, but Christ lives in me; and the life which I now live in the flesh I live by faith in the Son of God, who loved me and gave Himself up for me" (Gal. 2:20).

 6. *Lead students to join Christ in making disciples among all peoples.*

"Go therefore and make disciples of all the nations" (Matt. 28:19).

It is drudgery to call teenagers to live *for* Christ. It is thrilling to call teenagers to invite Christ to live His life *through* them.

There is a vast ocean of difference between trying to compel Christians to imitate Jesus and learning how to impart an implanted Christ. The former only ends up in failure and frustration. The latter is the gateway to life and joy in our daying and our dying. We stand with Paul: "Christ lives in me." Our life is Christ. In him do we live, breathe, and have our being. "What would Jesus do?" is not Christianity. Christianity asks: "What is Christ doing through me . . . through us? And how is Jesus doing it?" Following Jesus means "trust and obey" (respond), and living by his indwelling life through the power of the Spirit.[2]

Christ living His life through a teenager brings in His kingdom on earth and brings glory to Triune God. It is "Christ in you, the hope of glory" (Col. 1:27).

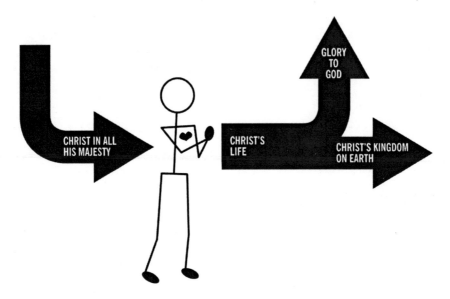

Three Common Criteria for Measuring the Effectiveness of Student Ministry

The criteria for any student ministry should be:

Are an increasing number of teenagers allowing the Christ they adore
to live out His life through them in ways that expand
His kingdom on earth,
make disciples of all nations, and bring glory to God?

But that is *not* the criteria for measuring student ministry effectiveness in most churches. Instead, three other criteria are more common.

① *Attendance*

Senior pastors, deacons/elders, personnel committees, parents, and other powerful people often evaluate the effectiveness of student ministry based on attendance. Some student ministers say, "Since I am not evaluated on any other measure than how many posteriors I put in chairs, then that is my primary focus whatever I plan."

2 Accolades and Absence of Complaints

Some key leaders in the church choose not to give the time that genuinely evaluating student ministry would take. Instead, they tend to form opinions about effectiveness based on whether members come to them with compliments or complaints. This can be dangerous in two directions. Member compliments (or just the absence of complaints) about a ministry that in reality is failing to build a sustainable faith in students can anesthetize any need for change.

On the other hand, member complaints can lead to negative pressure against a ministry just beginning to move in right directions. For example, parents whose offspring are missing the entertainment-only approach of the previous student minister might complain often enough to convince an uninformed pastor that something is wrong with the current ministry.

3 Comparison with Area Churches

Some powerful people in the church (including parents at times) evaluate ministry only as it seems to compare to area churches. "Well, our youth attendance is down, but that is what I am hearing from the other churches. I guess it is to be expected." "I see no reason for us not to have the same size youth group as my sister's church across town." "Other pastors talk about their on-fire student ministries, and I have no stories to tell."

Similar to the issue of accolades and criticisms, simply comparing ministry to other churches can lead to "false positive" and "false negative" evaluations. One student ministry that appears to be the biggest show in town may consistently be producing students who vaporize from the community of faith when the excitement of youth ministry is over. Another student ministry may get pounded in superficial comparisons but in reality may be producing students madly in love with Christ and committed to His purposes for a lifetime.

Just checking attendance, counting complaints, and making comparisons provide weak criteria for evaluating student ministry. It is time for all the stakeholders in student ministry to begin asking an entirely new set of questions.

The Real Question

- Are we seeing most collegians out of our student ministry quickly find a congregation with which to love and worship the Father?

- Are we seeing most young singles out of our student ministry increasingly embrace the full supremacy of the Son?

- Are we seeing most young couples out of our student ministry increasingly being conformed by the Spirit to Christ's image?

- Are we seeing most of those out of our student ministry live to make disciples for Christ among all peoples?

Many churches lose part of their youth group between middle school and high school, another part when students get cars and jobs, and another part during their senior year. Is it even realistic to imagine a student ministry where attendance, spiritual transformation, and passion actually *grow* every year? Does it make any sense to picture ministry where the strong faith of the seniors gives every evidence of lifetime sustainability? The short answer is yes!

Need proof it is possible? Here it is. For a select number of teenagers, student ministry *has* produced a growing, Christ-focused, sustainable faith across all six or seven years of student ministry. The intimacy and warmth of their relationship with Christ has grown even as their awe at His supremacy has mushroomed.

Student ministers must identify what "serum" worked for them and then quickly get it to the masses. The students who remain alive for Christ after youth group didn't get juicier pizzas or more exciting lock-ins. Much more likely is the probability those specific teenagers received, intentionally or unintentionally, ministry that looked similar to the following:

Foundational Principles for Student Ministry

1. Student ministry begins with a focus on the supremacy of Christ.

2. Students are most likely to embrace the full supremacy of Christ when they have heart connections with significant adults in their lives who increasingly embrace the full supremacy of Christ.

3. The highest priority in student ministry is leading parents and other adults who are significant to students increasingly to embrace the full supremacy of Christ.

4. The second highest priority in student ministry is leading students and the significant adults in their lives to build heart connections with each other—and then to live out the full supremacy of Christ together.

5. The third highest priority in student ministry is designing programming that allows students to build heart connections with peers and to live out the full supremacy of Christ together.

How Did We Get Where We Are?

Youth parachurch ministries created fifty or sixty years ago were birthed because the church was not effective in introducing to Christ those students outside the church. Young Bill Bright, Billy Graham, and others had hearts that ached for students who never were going to be reached by neat and tidy suburban churches.

Early parachurch leaders tended to be younger, creative, and relational. They were just right as missionaries to an unreached people group. Many of those parachurch ministries experienced visible success that caught the attention of church leaders. Church leaders began to imitate approaches from the parachurch groups without considering whether those models strategically were wise for the church. Soon most congregations were looking for someone young, creative, and relational around whom their teenagers could flock.

No one ever asked, "Is a model successful in reaching those outside the faith also the best model for building a sustainable faith centered on the majesty of Christ?" No one asked that question in the fifties when this pattern was becoming visible. Amazingly, no one began to ask the question in the turbulent sixties or for the forty years that followed.

Rather than changing what they were doing, leaders just tried to do what they were doing better. They assumed if teenagers benefited from flocking around a gifted youth leader, then they needed to allow more time for that. Positions went from part-time to full-time. Then leaders decided the students and that youth leader should share life out of town, so churches bought buses. Then churches built gyms so they could be together even more. And then state-of-the-art worship rooms. And then multimillion-dollar youth centers.

Those in student ministry have moved from the back of the plane to first class. They finally are enjoying eating good pasta instead of peanuts. But this book is the announcement that some student ministers are on the wrong plane headed to the wrong place. Does it really matter if leaders are in first class if they are headed in the wrong direction?

> Again, does it matter if leaders are in first class
> if they are headed in the wrong direction?

The Big Question

It all comes down to this central question: Are teenagers more likely to develop a sustainable faith embracing the full supremacy of Christ:

A. When they primarily relate to one youth leader and experience church almost exclusively with people their same age? Or,

B. When they build heart connections with several significant adults in their lives and they experience church in a rich web of intergenerational relationships?

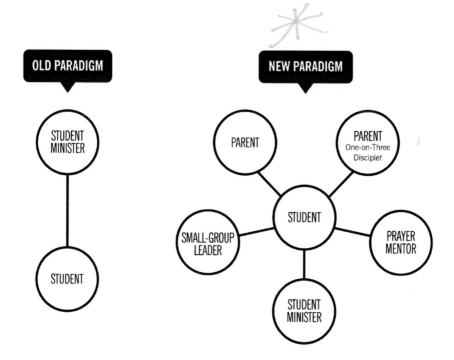

Five Alive

No one can say the church did not give the model on the left time to work. Sixty years is plenty of time for an experiment. Leaders can rejoice that over those decades *some* youth did embrace a walk with their King that sustained them into adulthood.

But *most* did not. And are not. And will not—unless change is made. It is time to move on.

Students who have heart connections with at least five significant, spiritually alive adults have the best opportunity to develop a sustainable, alive faith embracing the supremacy of Christ.

The heart of the Christian faith is a relationship—a relationship between Triune God and a believer as defined by the truth of Scripture. It should not be a surprise that relationships also are at the heart of spiritual transformation.

Why Five Relationships?

- Scripture is clear that father and mother are to be the primary spiritual leaders to teenagers. (See chapter 12 for the clear teaching of Scripture.)

- Research suggests teenagers also need a minimum of **three** adults outside the home to prosper emotionally and spiritually.[3]

Parents—No one has more potential than mom and dad to shape the spiritual life of a teenager. Scripture makes the point from cover to cover. A stack of research taller than a day-camp cooler supports the same conclusion.

Parents who are spiritually alive can serve as the primary discipler of their own children. Chapter 9 presents a plan for *one-on-three discipleship*—mobilizing many parents to disciple their own children and one or two others. Students whose parents cannot serve in this role need another godly adult to disciple them in life-on-life relationships.

Research also is converging on the importance of about three adults outside the home in shaping the spiritual and emotional development of teenagers. The three can be the student minister, small-group leader, and prayer mentor.

Student Minister—Student ministers always have been important to teenagers and to the kingdom. They will continue to be. In fact, they will become even more valuable as they seek to spark spiritual growth in the lives of adults who are important to teenagers, and they deepen the heart connections between teenagers and those adults. And all of this will add value even beyond the powerful impact student ministers have directly on teenagers, both through their public role and in integrity relationships.

Every statement in the preceding paragraph applies equally to unpaid, partially funded, and fully funded student ministers. The primary leader in any student ministry is valuable to teenagers.

Small-Group Leader—Churches have many different names for their primary Bible-teaching strategy for students (Sunday school, small-group Bible study, Bible study fellowship, etc). This book uses the term *open groups* to apply to all those approaches. The name comes from the fact the groups are always open to any student who shows interest in attending. Chapter 9 presents more detail about open groups. This book uses the term *small-group leader* to refer to those who lead open groups.

Every teenager needs a small-group leader who is living out and communicating truth, who is inviting him or her into deep prayer, and who is providing care and ministry. The life and teachings of this leader amplify and reinforce the voices of parents and others who disciple teenagers in one-on-three relationships.

For students not involved in one-on-three discipling, the small-group leader is the one member of the body of Christ (other than parents) most deeply committed to the spiritual well-being of the teenager. Because adults must balance many life responsibilities, most are not able to become involved life-on-life with more than about three students. Small-group leaders love all their members but only are able to invest life-on-life with their students *not* involved in one-on-three discipling.

Prayer Mentor—As chapter 13 will make clearer, teenage culture became an appendage to mainstream society for completely dysfunctional reasons. Parents who became consumed with their own issues mostly abandoned the young. Teenagers grasped one another for survival. It was *Lord of the Flies.* When the young figured out the adults mostly were gone, they had to build some sort of culture, even if it was filled with danger.

Somehow the church looked at that pathological development and decided it would be a dandy pattern for the church to follow. So for sixty years teenagers mostly have experienced church with people almost exactly their same age. The youth group is almost an appendage to the congregation. Watch the eyes of adults and teenagers as they pass in the halls at church. Not only do they not speak to each other, the two generations seem invisible to each other.

If the early church had adopted this model, then Acts 2:42-46 would read: "They devoted themselves to the apostles' teaching and to the fellowship, to the breaking of bread and to prayer, *with the adults in the upper room and the youth out in the stables.* Everyone was filled with awe, and many wonders and miraculous signs were done by the apostles, *but the teenagers missed this because they had a road trip.* All the believers were together, *well, the adults were together and the teenagers were together. . . .* Every day they continued to meet together in the temple courts *while the teenagers had a splash day.* They broke bread in their homes, *some homes for teenagers and some homes for adults."*

College freshman have dozens of reasons they begin sleeping in on Sunday morning for the first time in their lives. Among other things they may have no memory of feeling connected to a church congregation. Now that the youth group is no more, they may feel no hunger to replace adult bonds of the past with new ones in a new community of faith.

Making the youth group an appendage to the congregation did not work. This failed model resembles a famous cartoon mouse who must have lost an ear commuting between Orlando and Anaheim.

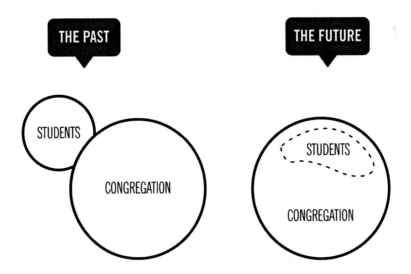

Teenagers who experience church in a rich web of intergenerational relationships are more likely to love and worship the Father, increasingly embrace the full supremacy of the Son, invite Christ to live His life through them, and join Him in making disciples among all peoples. The mouse's ear has got to go. It is time for change.

A major first step in reuniting the two generations is to pair a student with a member of the congregation in an integrity relationship. These pairs need a name. For many churches, the name *prayer mentor* might work well.

The efficacy of prayer always will be the center of a prayer mentor strategy. But prayer tends to bond hearts and can lead to a rich, life-altering relationship between a teenager and the adult who prays for him or her every day.

Prayer mentors tend to say, "You can't pray every day for young people without falling in love with them." Teenagers in those relationships tend to say, "I can't believe someone not in my family loves me enough to pray for me every day."

Mentors may move from concerted prayer to face-to-face relationships when they have the consent of parents, interest from the teenager, and completion of mentor training. Chapter 13 will focus on the *power of prayer* and what this might mean when each student has a committed intercessor or two. The discussion that follows will focus on the value of *a relationship* between a teenager and the adult who is praying for him or her.

Most adult prayer mentors are not student ministry volunteers in the traditional sense. Most never will sponsor trips or teach student Bible studies. And unlike disciplers, most never will meet teenagers at Starbucks. Prayer mentors use normal church life to build intentional relationships.

Prayer mentors are the answer to questions such as these:

- When a teenager walks into the auditorium, which adult is the first to show delight?

- Which adult is likely to hand a teenager a laminated clipping when the teenager's name is in the paper?

- Which adult finds the teenager at the church potluck to breathe a prayer for her mother's chemo?

And their teenage prayer partners are the answer to questions such as these:

- When an adult walks through the gym, which teenager is the first to show delight?

- Which teenager shows up just in time to fold the wheelchair for the trunk?

- Which teenager sits with the adult at the church potluck while his wife is in the hospital?

Prayer mentors are always good for a hug after a hard week. And birthday cards show up. And students get mail while on a mission trip. A teenager gets out of school to go to the prayer mentor's funeral and sits up front with the family. And it's the *whole* church just being the church.

This strategy goes far beyond just connecting one student with one member of the congregation. This strategy can lead to reimmersing the full youth group in the full congregation. The following background can make this statement believable.

Chap Clark's research has discovered that teenagers tend to form gender-specific clusters of approximately four to eight members. Teenagers often view their cluster as essential to their survival.

Here is an important fact. Teenagers will accept as trustworthy any adult who a member of their cluster says is trustworthy. Therefore, when a student in your church forms a heart connection with a prayer mentor, then that adult can slowly become valuable to all the members of the student's cluster.

At the same time, all of the other members of the cluster are growing in relationship with *their* prayer mentors and introducing their mentors to the cluster. Thus, the number of linkages between the generations can increase exponentially over time. The mouse might lose that one ear in months rather than decades.

Parents without Christ

Students who have heart connections with at least five significant, spiritually alive adults have the *best* opportunity to develop a sustainable, alive faith that embraces the supremacy of Christ. But what about the large percentage of teenagers in most churches whose parents do not know Christ? All the research says they *almost* are destined to leave the church in late high school or certainly after graduation. They are dangling by a thread.

Baring an outright miracle, their only hope for a sustainable faith is *at least* three heart connections with spiritually alive adults who hold to them tenaciously. If they have not found those relationships, sirens should be going off and warning lights flashing.

Simplest Student Ministry

Based on the discussions above, here may be the simplest way to describe the weekly flow of student ministry. These components compliment the spiritual leadership of parents in the home and are strengthened through the intercession of prayer mentors.

> *Corporate and Student Worship*—Presenting worship with the full body of Christ as primary and normative for all believers.
>
> *Open-Group Bible Study*—Introducing students to Christ, connecting them to the church, teaching them foundational concepts of God's Word, and ministering to their needs.
>
> *One-on-Three Discipleship*—Taking the next step in the spiritual journey.
>
> *Fellowship*—Forming and deepening relationships and celebrating the abundant life.
>
> *Evangelism/Ministry/Missions*—Both being and doing. Both personal and corporate. Both planned and spontaneous.

Church Schedules

Some student ministers might reject new paradigms for youth ministry by saying, "I can see the value in some new approaches, but unfortunately our schedule here will not permit those changes." The proverbial tail may be wagging the dog. Schedules are not sacred, nor do they flow from holy writ.

First you determine the mission of a church or a student ministry. Then you determine which gatherings will best achieve that mission.

Then you determine a schedule for those gatherings most likely to help you achieve your mission.

Closing

There is no formula. Student ministry has no guarantees. Students are free moral agents. One can live in rich relationships with five spiritually alive adults and still choose faithlessness. It is rare but it can happen.

And miracles happen. Students with pagan parents and no caring adults in their lives can meet Jesus and embrace Him and His mission for a lifetime. It is not the norm but it can happen. Christ is not limited by diagrams and paradigms.

But it is *much* more likely students will spend a lifetime embracing the full supremacy of the Son, responding to His majesty in all of life, inviting Christ to live His life through them, and joining Him in making disciples among all peoples when they are immersed in relationships with believers who already are on that journey.

In summary, student ministers increasingly desire:

- To see teenagers awakened to the full supremacy of the Son of God.

- To see teenagers adore Christ as they discover and embrace more of who He truly is.

- To see teenagers inviting Christ to live His life through them and joining Him in making disciples among all peoples.

- To see teenagers lead the full church into an awakening to Christ for all He is today.

Student ministers increasingly believe these outcomes are more likely:

- When parents awakened to the supremacy of Christ serve as the primary spiritual leaders to their own children.

- When student ministers and the other vocational ministers of the church live out before teenagers their own awakening to the Son of God.

- When volunteers awakened to the supremacy of Christ disciple and mentor teenagers in integrity relationships.

- When members of the congregation awakened to the supremacy of Christ envelope teenagers in warm and caring relationships.

- When teenagers awakened to the supremacy of Christ live in biblical community with their peers.

That's Just the Big Picture

This chapter has provided only a helicopter view of a new paradigm for student ministry. It will take the remainder of the book even to begin to sketch out the implications.

Chapter Six
Strategic Planning

Under the old paradigm, student ministers usually emerged from their office with finished calendars. Why? Some thought this was what they were being paid to do. (And sometimes they were right.) Some could not find anyone else to help. Some wanted freedom to do what they wanted to do without other opinions. Some wanted to prop up their self-esteem by creating the impression only they were wise enough to plan student ministry.

Why is this not the best plan?

- *Doctrine*—Student ministry belongs to the church so some expression of the congregation should be involved in crafting it.

- *Intelligence*—Several are almost always smarter than one. This is vital since a new paradigm will require rethinking all of student ministry.

- *Motivation*—What you design, others will allow you to make happen. What others design, they will join you in preparing.

- *Communication*—What you design, you must sell alone. What others design, they will join you in selling.

- *Training*—If you plan alone, no one will know how during the months following your leaving. If others plan with you, they learn to design consistent ministry as staff members come and go.

 Overview of Strategic Planning

1. Lead a purpose statement design team (several core students, parents, and volunteers) to define a purpose statement for your student ministry.

2. Lead your student ministry to own the purpose statement.

3. Design a concrete way for students, parents, and youth staff to evaluate present student ministry in light of the purpose statement.

4. Create a core planning team to shape your plan for the coming year.

5. Guide the core planning team to digest the concrete evaluation of student ministry.

6. In light of that analysis, guide the core planning team to set several high priorities for the coming year.

7. Choose ministry responses (programs, events, ministries, etc.) to those high priorities, being careful to identify a primary student ministry purpose and target audience for each.

8. Consider your people, time, and financial resources as you choose responses.

9. Move the ministry responses you have chosen to twelve balanced calendars.

10. Create lead teams to implement each major programming element.

More Detail about Strategic Planning

Prayer—One of the most common and most dangerous statements made in the church today is, "Somebody please open us in a quick prayer so we can get started."

For believers who are waking up to the supreme majesty of Christ, that statement ought to sound like long fingernails clawing an old blackboard. It is close to saying, "Let's get this ritual over with as quickly as possible so we can get on with applying our human intelligence to planning good student ministry."

Jesus prayed all night before He chose the first apostles. You should pray a *long* time before enlisting the team that will shape the purpose statement.

The early church in Acts prayed deeply (and even fasted on occasion) before making major decisions. When your team convenes, deep prayer should be a central agenda item.

You don't just lengthen the prayer time by taking prayer requests and then praying for grandmother's gout. You adore and magnify Triune God. You confess sin. You proclaim gratitude for blessings. Then you cry out for wisdom to know the mind of Christ in setting a purpose statement for your student ministry.

When that work is finished, you go back on your knees to discover who Christ has chosen for the core planning team. Then you give more time planning how you will lead them to pray than planning any other part of the agenda. You might even weave together prayer, Scripture, and song to prepare their hearts for planning.

Later, when they complete the evaluation, they thank God for the insights He provided and then ask for wisdom for the next step. When they complete the priorities for the new year, they pause for more prayers of thanks and more prayers for the mind of Christ. When they complete *each* item of the agenda, the process is the same.

Later, every lead team should follow the same pattern. You should be more careful to teach chairpersons how to lead group prayer than you are to teach them how to lead a good meeting.

The Student Minister—When following the new paradigm of student ministry, you link arms with students, parents, and volunteers to establish a purpose statement and to do strategic planning. But shared leadership does not diminish your importance to the process.

In both sets of meetings, you may have done the most careful study of Scripture related to the task. You may be the most widely read in the field, and you may have the most formal or informal training. Your passion for Christ, for students, and for student ministry may motivate you to spend the most hours a week thinking carefully about this arena of ministry. You may have had positive and negative experiences in previous churches that shed light on planning.

Shared leadership does not call into question your competence. In fact, it takes much more competence to equip and guide the saints to craft student ministry than it does to do unilateral planning in your office with the door closed.

Define a Purpose Statement—Doug Fields has laid out an excellent approach to defining a purpose statement.

- Work with the pastor and other church leaders to clarify the direction your church is heading so the student ministry purpose statement will work in harmony with it.

- Teach the team shaping the purpose statement the biblical foundation for the five student ministry purposes (see below).

- Invite the team to express their thoughts and to suggest words and phrases.

- Compose the final statement.

- If the church has a purpose statement, ensure the student ministry purpose statement clearly flows from it.

- Request support from the pastor for the new statement.

- Launch the purpose statement with wisdom.[1]

Own the Purpose Statement—Again, no one can improve on Doug Field's suggestions for getting your new purpose statement into the DNA of students, parents, volunteers, and congregation. Here is a brief summary:

- Challenge key students and adults to memorize the statement.

- Teach on the statement and ask your staff to do so.

- Make your statement visible with a poster or banner.

- Print the statement on letters and calendars.

- Review the statement at meetings of parents and volunteers.

- Show parents, volunteers, and church leaders that every program supports a purpose.

- Invite each stakeholder in student ministry to pray for one of the purposes.[2]

Evaluate—This might be a standardized evaluation from a publisher. It might be notes from a "town hall" meeting with student ministry stakeholders that solicited feedback. It might be focus groups. It could be your idea that's better than any of these.

Core Planning Team—This team usually is composed of core students, parents, and volunteers who are spiritually transformed and sensitive to the Spirit's leading, who have the purpose statement in their DNA, and who are adept in strategic planning. Since the church has called the student minister to take the lead in shaping its student ministry, he chairs this team.

As the team considers ministry to and with students, it is important to have students in the conversation. As the team considers the needs of parents, it makes sense that parents are on the team. As the team plans to empower and equip volunteers in entirely new ways, the voices of some of those volunteers need to be heard.

Student Ministry Purposes—Student ministry and the full church share the same functions: discipleship, evangelism, fellowship, ministry, and worship. (Notice they are listed in alphabetical order to avoid the debate about which comes first and which is most important). Missions is the melding of evangelism and ministry.

The goal of each of the five student ministry purposes is students who, for the glory of the Father and in the power of the Spirit, spend a lifetime embracing the full supremacy of the Son, responding to His majesty in all of life, inviting Christ to live His life through them, and joining Him in making disciples among all peoples.

Ministry Responses—*Ministry responses* is an umbrella term to include all the core planning team plans to address priorities for the new year. Responses include programs, events, and ministries. Under the new student ministry paradigm, some programming will target specific subsets of students, some will target parents, some will target volunteers, and some will target the congregation. Some will target students and their parents, some will target students and their volunteer leaders, some will target students and members of the congregation, and some will target volunteer leaders and parents.

Target Audiences

- *Community Students*—Students in a realistic driving distance of your church. They have no commitment to Christ or your church.

- *Crowd Students*—Students who attend your large gathering weekly. They can be Christians or non-Christians.

- *Congregation Students*—Students committed to a small group. They have a relationship with Christ and with other Christians.

- *Committed Students*—Students who are committed to developing such spiritual disciplines as personal Bible study, prayer, accountability with another believer, Scripture memorization, giving, and commitment to the full church body.

- *Core Students*—Students who discover their gifts and express them through ministry.[3]

- *Non-Christian Parents of Your Students*

- *Christian Parents of Your Students*

- *Volunteers Who Teach Groups*

- *Volunteers Who Disciple*

- *Members of the Congregation*

You and the core planning team should be able to state the primary student ministry function and the primary target audience for every event, project, and ministry on the student ministry calendar.

Lead Teams—Lead teams serve to implement events or projects calendared by the core planning team. Examples include youth camp, a retreat, an all-night prayer gathering, or a family remodeling project at the rescue mission. Lead teams serve to implement events or projects according to a design and spirit affirmed by the core planning team and consistent with the vision and direction of the entire congregation.

Lead teams are composed of students, parents of students, and volunteers. Lead teams generally have four to twelve members. Lead teams are assembled to accomplish a particular task or mission and exist only long enough to fulfill that objective.

Lead teams should not be confused with groups or committees who "help the student minister" with an event. Lead teams accept ultimate responsibility for their event or project. The student minister serves to motivate, inspire, and give general direction to their work, but the team has ultimate responsibility.

Teams do not do all the work on events and projects. They may involve many members in their work. They simply take the lead, coordinating role.

Possible Structure of a Lead Team in a Smaller Church

Student	Seasoned student ministry volunteer—chairperson
Student	Parent

Possible Structure of a Lead Team in a Larger Church

Student	Seasoned student ministry volunteer—chairperson
Student	Student ministry volunteer
Student	Student ministry volunteer
Student	Parent
Student	Parent
Student	Parent

The Purpose of Lead Teams

1. To assist the student minister in moving to a leadership style that emphasizes equipping the saints to do the work of the ministry, in the spirit of Ephesians 4:11–12.

2. To enable the student minister to shift time from event and project management to higher priorities.

3. To open opportunities for students, parents, and volunteers to express fully their giftedness as they arise to join Christ in His kingdom activity.

4. To allow the church and the kingdom to experience the benefits flowing from the saints and the student minister each expressing their unique calling and function in ministry.

Chairpersons

Before enlisting the chairperson of each team, the student minister will want to spend time praying deeply. That selection cannot be left to chance. The selection of the chairperson may be the most important variable in the effectiveness of lead team ministry. Chairpersons must be seasoned student ministry volunteers who have a clear vision of the events and projects they are creating. They must be fully supportive of the student minister and share a heart for ministry.

Organizing Teams

Team members increasingly in awe of Christ will desire His direction in joining a team. Here is one way to accomplish that.

1. Assemble students, parents of students, and volunteers.

2. Display large posters, each labeled with a lead team event or project and the respective chairpersons.

3. Lightly tape to each poster note cards that represent the positions available for that team. That might mean four cards that say "Student," two that say "Parent," and one that says "Student Ministry Volunteer."

4. Overview each lead team event or project.

5. Invite those present to ask Christ's guidance in making a first choice or second choice for team membership. Since perfunctory public prayers are not adequate for this

purpose, invite those present to choose a prayer partner for concerted prayer.

6. Ask each student, parent, and volunteer to take an appropriate card from one of the posters. If they should find all the appropriate cards gone from one poster, ask them to go to another poster to find a position. (Make sure the number of positions available is about equal to the number of students, parents, and volunteers present. If the group is smaller than anticipated, remove posters. If the group is larger than expected, add posters that have been prepared for just this possibility. Too few posters mean willing workers go unused. Too many posters mean teams too small to get their work done.)

7. Prepare team rosters based on the cards that have been taken. Add contact information to the rosters to aid communication.

8. Invite new teams to assemble briefly for fellowship, prayer, and initial dreaming. Announce when teams will begin their work.

Meeting Times and Places

Most churches will experience greater success when lead teams meet simultaneously. Consider these advantages.

- The youth minister can spend the entire time going team to team, offering encouragement, solving problems, and ensuring the quality of plans underway.

- When teams meet at the same time, attendance is more visible, and team members feel more accountable to attend.

- Members feel more excitement when they see a larger number of team members at work.

- Potential schedule or resource conflicts between teams can be solved easily.

In order to secure the advantages listed above, team meetings should be held as close to one another as is practical. Meeting around tables in a fellowship hall may permit teams to see one another at work yet not disturb other teams.

If possible, team-meeting times should be tied to other weekly church events. Most team members prefer meeting Sunday noon, Sunday afternoon or evening, or Wednesday evening over coming out on a weeknight or Saturday. Ministers need to protect a prime meeting time for lead teams each month, without conflicts.

Monthly simultaneous meetings will be about right for most churches. Teams quickly approaching their event may decide to plan additional meetings or work sessions.

A team chairperson and the student minister should decide how many months before an event a team should begin meeting. Complicated projects such as an out-of-state mission trip may require a six-month head start. A simple activity at the church may require only two months.

Time Line

Churches must discover the best time line for their situation. Here are three options.

1. Organize all lead teams for the year at the same time. After membership on all teams is set, announce when each team will begin meeting during the year (typically from two to six months before their event or project). Allow team members to rest after they complete their assignment.

2. Organize lead teams at the beginning of each quarter. Organize teams that will lead events not during that quarter but in the quarter to follow. (For example, organize teams in September that will lead events from December to February or March).

3. Assemble students, parents, and volunteers and organize a specific lead team when it is time for that team to begin meeting.

When considering the above options, the basic questions are: How long do we want team members to have off before we challenge them to join a new team? When they finish their work, do we want them to be off until the beginning of the new church year? Until the beginning of the next quarter? Do we have so few youth and adults that we need them to begin a new team assignment right away? Each church's situation will be different.

Budget Administration

Each lead team chairperson needs clear guidance on the money his or her team has to spend. The easiest way to communicate this is with budget line items for lead team events. Chairpersons quickly can see the amounts they have to spend. Since budget reports are public, chairpersons tend to take those limits seriously.

Quality Control

You care about the quality of programming provided for teenagers, parents, and volunteers. It is painful to watch something done poorly. Leaders considering the lead team concept may honestly wonder, *How do I know teams actually will do quality work?*

There are no guarantees. However, teams in scores of churches across the nation are indeed providing first-class events, activities, and projects. Most don't want to be associated with leading a flop. Much more importantly, most want to maximize their impact for the kingdom.

You can monitor the quality of planning in at least three ways. First, you can move from team to team during the regularly scheduled team meeting sessions. Visiting informally with a team provides some sense of how they are progressing in their plans. No team wants a third-degree grilling, but light questions are not offensive and provide the feedback you need.

You also need to observe whether teams are making prayer the foundation of their planning. The statement, "Let's open our meeting with a quick word of prayer" is inconsistent with the supremacy of Christ. If He is supreme and has all the wisdom the team needs for their work, then concerted prayer toward Him is the most important item on the agenda. Chairpersons need to call the team to a season of prayer when they assemble and before each major decision.

Second, you can request a copy of each team's minutes at the end of meeting times. It is much easier to get minutes copied as teams are dismissing than some time later in the week. Team minutes provide important feedback concerning both the quality and the direction of the team's planning.

Third, you can stay in touch with chairpersons informally between scheduled team meetings. Church hallway conversations, phone calls, and even lunches together provide valuable feedback. Once again, no one enjoys an FBI-styled questioning. Instead, you can initiate conversations with questions such as: Can I help you with any information about your retreat? Do you need any help from the ministers? Gentle questions in the context of offering help and showing interest generally lead to the feedback the student minister needs.

Making the Case for Lead Teams

To motivate others to consider lead teams, you can make the following points during a group presentation:

The Bible suggests a better way for us to organize our student ministry. Lead the group in a word-by-word study of Ephesians 4:11–12. Compare the reading of the King James Version (which is easy to misunderstand) and newer translations. Emphasize that vocational ministers are given gifts primarily to be used in equipping the saints so the saints can perform the work of the ministry. Use commentaries and Bible study tools to prepare a thorough study. Explain that the goal is to organize student ministry closer to the New Testament pattern.

A better way to organize our student ministry would allow us to expand and move into any areas where we sense God is at work. Explain that with the present organization, adding new ministries is difficult. You may even want to say that because you are basically in charge of everything, you simply don't have time to consider adding new programs or ministries.

Present the possibility of introducing a way to organize that would allow the church to respond quickly to new needs and opportunities that emerge and to begin new ministries in response to seeing where God is at work.

Such a plan would allow the student minister to move into new areas of ministry. Here you can help the group see the need for you to begin to spend more time:

- Embracing personally and living out the supremacy of Christ.

- Linking arms with other spiritual leaders to lead significant adults in the lives of students to embrace the majesty of Christ.

- Linking arms with other spiritual leaders to lead significant adults in the lives of students to build heart connections with those students.

- Guiding spiritually sensitive students, parents, and volunteers in designing programming that allows students and adults to live out the supremacy of Christ together.

- Guiding spiritually sensitive students, parents, and volunteers in designing programming that allows students to build heart connections with peers and to experience biblical community.

Hundreds of churches are adopting a strategy that is New Testament in design, allows them to move into many new areas of student ministry, and allows their student ministers to give more attention to their highest priorities in ministry. At this point present the lead team strategy. Adapt the strategy to fit the church's situation. Use handouts and visuals to aid communication. Allow open discussion and provide positive answers to questions that may arise. If the group seems open to the strategy, enthusiastically announce what the next step toward implementation will be.

Closing

Strategic planning looks boring to some. But not when it's done by,

people of Christ, through Christ, and for Christ. A people of the cross. A people who are consumed with God's eternal passion, which is to make his Son preeminent, supreme, and the head over all things visible and invisible. A people who have discovered the touch of the Almighty in the face of his glorious Son. A people who wish to know only Christ and him crucified, and to let everything else fall by the wayside. A people who are laying hold of his depths, discovering his riches, touching his life, and receiving his love, and making HIM in all of his unfathomable glory known to others.[4]

Chapter Seven
Prayer, Worship, and Fellowship

Good for you! Others probably look at this chapter title and then skip it for the chapters that are more "practical and useful." You know better. You know an awakening to Christ without prayer will never happen. You also know true awakening always will lead to adoring Christ in worship in powerful new ways. And that depth of worship leads to deeper unity and fellowship in the body.

Prayer

Every believer knows prayer is important. At the same time . . .

Prayer is not the answer. Christ is the answer.

The power is not in prayer. The power is in Christ.

Prayer does not bring awakening. The Father leads the church into an awakening to His Son.

But because prayer is conversation and union with Triune God, its importance cannot be overstated.

God gives you a vision for families, student ministries, and churches so wonderful you conclude you cannot live without it. But then He helps you realize it is so wonderful you cannot personally produce it. Can't live without it; can't produce it? That's when you must conclude your primary option is to seek it—to pray.

True prayer is not an effort to get Christ to do something. It is a desire to be in union with Him.

Because of grace you may boldly approach the throne. As you ascend the steps, an absolutely remarkable thing happens—the King of the universe stands up. Not only that, but He motions for you to come close. He wraps His strong arms around you and draws your head to His chest. You can hear His heartbeat. The longer you are with Him, the more your heart beats as His does. You begin to see reality the way He does. His thoughts become your thoughts. His passions become your passions. Then, when you begin to intercede, you simply are expressing what you have discovered to be His heart.

Prayer is the prelude to a fresh work of God. As you call on Him to come and do what you cannot do for yourself, prayer makes room for Jesus to take center stage. When you use phrases such as "in Jesus' name," "for Jesus' sake," or "for Christ's glory alone" in your prayers, you signal your desire for God to unleash His promises in a way that opens wide the door for more of Christ and His supremacy.

When you pray, "Your kingdom come, Your will be done on earth as it is in heaven," you lobby the Throne of the universe to give fullest expression to every facet of Christ's lordship. You appeal to the Father to stamp the nature and character of His Son on every facet of student ministry.

The Student Minister's Prayer Life

With few exceptions prayer will not saturate a student ministry until it saturates the student minister.

On May 3, 2006, I listened as Becky Tirabassi challenged those attending the Youth Ministry Executive Council meeting near Washington, D.C. She told us the story of the 1947 Fellowship of the Burning Heart, which began as a gathering of passionate students and leaders who determined to live "sold out" lives for God for ALL of their lives. The original Fellowship included a young businessman by the name of Bill Bright who went on to found Campus Crusade for Christ. Those collegians made a clear declaration to Christ that they would live sexually pure lives and would spend a minimum of an hour in prayer every morning for the rest of their lives.

As Becky continued speaking, my mind had to stop and deal with this thought: *For some reason, I am sitting in this roomful of national leaders in student ministry. Even though my ministry platform is not as expansive as some, I do equip student ministers, and I do share life with teenagers in my church. If collegians from a previous generation desired to be before their Monarch at least an hour every morning, would I want to be there less?* I quietly bowed my head and told the Son of God there would never be a morning I would spend less than an hour in His holy presence. I cannot begin to describe the changes in my life and my heart that have flowed from these luxurious times with Jesus. Now the morning time spills into a running conversation with my Regent throughout the day.

Spending an hour in morning prayer and Scripture is neither biblical nor normative. Many saints through the ages have spent multiplied hours a day. Others have been invited to pray more briefly. The issue is not the length of prayer but the consistency and the depth.

Student ministers might ask Christ, "Is there any minimum length of time You would invite me to be before You each morning? Would it please You if I were to promise You I would be before You at least that long—every morning until the day I die? Would You send Your Spirit to give me resolve never to waver from this promise? Would You so dazzle me with Your glory that I will look forward to every chance to stand before You?"

Prayer-saturated student ministries tend to flow from prayer-saturated student ministers. The opposite also is true. Student ministers tend to get prayer saturated when they spend time with prayer-saturated people.

Prayer Strategies

If you make perfect preparations for a hayride but forget the truck, how will the evening go? If you make perfect preparations for an international mission trip but forget transportation, what will the group think standing on the church parking lot? If you make full preparation for student ministry but forget prayer, do you really think life-changing spiritual impact still will be the result?

Consider these diagnostic questions:

- What is your next big event in student ministry?
- What actions have you taken to prepare for this event?

- How many total hours have been spent in preparation by all leaders?

- To this point, what actions have been taken to call the church and/or student ministry to prayer over this event?

- How many minutes has the youth group spent in concerted prayer over this event?

- How have parents and volunteers been invited to pray that Christ's kingdom will come on earth through this event?

Are you comfortable with your answers to these questions?

Most families, student ministries, and churches speak more about prayer than they pray. One of the first signs of an awakening to Christ will be the multiplication of true prayer everywhere believers live and worship. Here are just a few of many ways prayer may seep into the DNA of student ministry.

Intercession during Student Ministry Gatherings—Consider inviting intercessors to pray during student ministry gatherings. Place blank cards in chairs before students arrive. As the gathering begins, invite students to write signed or unsigned prayer requests. Collect the cards and then take them to the intercessors. Ensure students know intercessors are bringing their requests before the heavenly throne even while the gathering continues. Intercessors can be students or adults.

Prayer as a Part of Student Ministry Gatherings—Few leaders would allow someone with poor theology to speak or lead a Bible study for a large gathering of students. The same care should be exercised when inviting students and adults to lead public prayer. Those whose public prayers are laundry lists of requests for Christ to fulfill but include no adoration of Him simply perpetuate seeing Jesus as a mascot. Those whose public prayers imply Jesus quickly needs to remove any illness, suffering, or hardship perpetuate bad theology. On the other hand, those who lead public prayers focused on the majesty of Christ and *His* divine plans can help guide the prayers of all worshippers.

Public prayers have a biblical place in corporate worship gatherings. One complement to public prayers is small-group prayer. Since teenagers tend to have shorter attention spans, most can feel more engaged in prayer that directly involves them. Even in large venues, wise leaders may say, "Please stand and quickly form a small group with three or four around you. If you do not pray out loud, you may remain silent while the others in your small group pray aloud. Speaking in sentence prayers, I want you to adore the majesty of the Son of God until you hear the music begin."

Large worship gatherings likely will include students who do not yet have a relationship with Jesus Christ. Will small-group prayer offend them? Not likely. In fact, this generation of students is fascinated with spiritual practices. Even if they do not participate, pre-Christians may be intrigued as they listen to others speak to the Son of God in a personal way.

The other complement to public prayers is silent prayer. Students and adults need to learn to quiet their souls before the living Lord of glory. They need to become comfortable in the courts of the Royal Highness. In stillness they need to hear His voice, and they need to proclaim His grandeur.

Prayer Bracelets—Consider purchasing hospital identification bracelets from a medical supply company. Place on the bracelets the names of all students, parents, and leaders who will be involved in some ministry or trip. Invite members of the congregation to wear a bracelet leading up to and during the ministry or trip. Ask them to pray for the individual listed each time they see the bracelet. Also ask them to solicit additional prayers from those who ask about the bracelet. Prepare a printed guide for each person who takes a bracelet. Provide specific suggestions for prayer. For example, consider including the daily schedule for the ministry or trip so the intercessor can pray more targeted prayers.

Twenty-Four-Hour Prayer Vigils—Consider calling the student group, parents, volunteers, or the congregation to twenty-four hours of prayer. (A twenty-four-hour prayer vigil would be an excellent way to launch the new student ministry paradigm presented in this book.) Enlist intercessors who each will pray for thirty minutes. Provide each intercessor a printed guide for prayer. (Sadly, many in the church today do not know how to pray thirty minutes without clear direction.) In some neighborhoods it is safe for intercessors to come to the church to pray even during the night. In other neighborhoods this would be impossible. If intercessors need to pray in their own homes during the night, invite the person completing thirty minutes of prayer to call the next person—for unity, continuity of prayer, and accountability.

Prayer Rooms during Events—Consider creating a prayer room during every major student ministry event, conference, and convention. If practical, add a rug, kneeling rail, and visual focal point (cross, portrait, etc.). Provide soft, instrumental music (lyrics sometimes distract prayer). Provide Bibles, printed prayer guides, and prayer requests specific to the gathering. Enlist intercessors who will pray during the entire gathering. Also consider letting all at the gathering know they can go to the prayer room at any time for private prayer or to pray with an intercessor.

Prayer Rooms Year-Round—Consider creating a permanent prayer room in the student ministry area at church. (If you have room for video games and snacks but no room for prayer, you might be sending students a message you did not intend to send.) Since chairs are optional, choose a floor covering comfortable for sitting or kneeling. Consider a permanent kneeling rail facing a focal point. Create a simple way for those who come to turn on instrumental worship music. Consider allowing each wall to represent a different focus for prayer. For example, one wall could feature a floor-to-ceiling map of the world and could be the focus for global praying. Building supply companies now are carrying a black-paint product that turns a wall into a blackboard. Students could use this surface to write requests and answers to prayer in chalk. String and clothespins running the length of a wall can hold prayer requests and answers as well. Provide Bibles, printed prayer guides, and art supplies so students can express and display insights that come in prayer.

An Empty Chair—Consider from time to time using an empty chair to symbolize Christ enthroned. In small-group settings invite students one at a time to sit or kneel before the chair, seeking to visualize Christ enthroned as they adore Him and make intercession before Him. In corporate worship occasionally relocate musicians out of site and place the chair alone on the platform. Invite worshippers to direct all prayers and singing to the One who sits at the right hand of the Father.

If you are a vocational minister, consider adding an empty chair at the head of the table during staff meetings. Direct prayers to the true Chairman of the board before planning. Later, before making important decisions, direct attention back to Him and His desires for your church.

Invite parents and volunteers occasionally to add an empty chair to their workstations during the week. Challenge them to stay in constant conversation with the King seated in their cubicle or nurses station.

Suggestions

1. When groups gather to pray, invite them to pray on one theme at a time. (For example: adoration, confession, thanksgiving, and intercession). Ask each person to pray aloud many times but briefly each time. When a petition is offered, invite one or two others to pray in agreement with that petition.

2. When someone shares a prayer request with the group and then later offers prayer over that issue, this takes twice as much time. Invite group members not to share prayer requests with the group. Instead, ask them to begin praying aloud about their concern. Assure them the group will care about the issue and several will agree with them in prayer.

3. Teach prayer groups to welcome silence and to use it to commune with Christ.

4. Teach students, parents, and volunteers the difference between prayers of praise and prayers of gratitude. Because of the current crisis in Christology, many believers do not know how to compose expressions of praise and adoration.

5. Show prayer groups how to pray Scripture and how to move easily from speaking prayers to singing prayers.

6. Remind students, parents, and volunteers that church chairs have no seat belts. Invite them to stand, keel, or fall prostrate before the Lamb of God.

7. Gently move away from opening and closing prayers that are just rote expressions uttered while group members daydream. Clarify the purpose of every prayer and think of new ways to draw each person into conversation with King Jesus.

8. When students come to you one-on-one with a prayer request, they may be thinking you have an inside track with God that gives your prayers more power. You might respond to their sharing by saying something like, "I want you to know I care that you are facing this challenge. But in reality I am just human, and I don't have the power to bring change to this situation. But you know who does. So just begin now expressing your concern to Christ. After you have prayed, then I will join in and will express agreement with your desire to see Christ glorified in the situation." This approach quietly teaches students in any life challenge that they should approach Christ first rather than last.

In Summary

All prayer is about extending the supremacy of Christ from here to eternity. Therefore, all prayers to the Father about the kingdom can be distilled into one word: *Come!* And all answers boil down to one person: *Christ!*

Worship

Undistracted Worship

The Jewish temple had concentric courtyards. Only the priests could enter the inner courtyard. Only Jewish men could enter the next one out, and only Jewish women the next one. The most outer courtyard was designated for Gentile God fearers. For non-Jewish worshippers with hearts for God, this was their only place of corporate worship.

That is why it made Jesus angry that Jewish entrepreneurs had robbed the God fearers of their place of worship by making it into a noisy market. Soon He was taking matters in His own hands, turning tables upside down and scattering the merchandise.

Spiritual leaders of students need to have the mind of Christ related to worship. You need to make worship as undistracted as possible in order that students can focus on the exalted Christ.

Similar to the first century, marketers and entrepreneurs have moved into places of worship. In the local church the camp promo video runs right between worship songs. At large rallies and conferences, the speaker's newest book fills a thirty-foot Jumbotron as he speaks. If worshippers consider lifting their hands to heaven, they must first do something with all the promo literature they were handed as they arrived.

As you fall more in love with Jesus, you increasingly will want students to be able to stand before His throne without being distracted. For local student worship this may mean placing a clear break between icebreakers and program promotion and the beginning of worship. It also may mean enlisting only worship musicians and leaders who want all the focus on the Son. On some occasions the band might be a silhouette while a cross is spotlighted. Or the band might be at the rear of the room. Any time students rush the stage, it should be to fall prostrate before His Majesty.

In terms of big concerts, rallies, and conferences, you must be the shepherd for your flock. Many students will not be transformed enough to know how to choose which events to attend. When you sense ahead of time that one conference will saturate worship with product tables, handouts, and platform announcements, you may well decide to bypass it for an event where you know Christ will be exalted without those distractions. When you see one concert that will feature a band preoccupied with its greatness and another concert with a band who desires all eyes on Christ, you just shepherd your flock to know which to attend.

As you teach and lead, you will see your students and leaders begin to hunger for Christ alone. Someday your group may attend a big conference and unexpectedly hear the singer say, "While I sing this next song, I want you to kneel before Jesus in your mind's eye. I hope this song blesses you since it is on my new CD, which will be in stores

71

on Tuesday or at my product table tonight." At that moment you may glance down the row to see most of your students in prayer, silently asking Christ to give the artist a hunger for Him and for undistracted worship.

Worship and Hope in Christ

Believers worship more accurately and more passionately when they do so in hope. Not only do they praise Him for who He is or what He has done, but believers also celebrate what He's getting ready to do. Students can rejoice ahead of time over displays of Christ's dominion they know are promised. After all, He is not only the God who is and was but also the God who is to come (Rev. 1). Student worship should say so!

Properly understood, worship is designed not only to be Christ centered but also heaven centered. Students, families, and churches should worship in a way that prepares them for the worship they expect to experience in His presence for the rest of eternity. In other words, they are called to preview the kind of worship into which the entire universe has been invited!

Furthermore, hope-filled worship transforms every other aspect of discipleship. Take, for example, missions. Worship among the nations is actually a "preview of coming attractions" of the hour not long from now when people from every tongue, tribe and peoples will shout their redemption before Him who sits on the throne and before the Lamb (Rev. 5). True worship, therefore, must stir up in students and their parents and leaders a greater determination to extend His praises among friends or neighbors or unreached peoples. All evangelism is ultimately about expanding eternal adoration for God's Son into the midst of those who do not yet know Him.

The heart of every student minister should skip a beat when Rick Lawrence asks, "Can you imagine the joy you'd taste if you could answer 'adoration' when others innocently ask you what makes your ministry 'successful'? Teenagers caught up in the pursuit and adoration of Jesus will live and breathe and move in the spirit of the first disciples—the same ones who started to believe that if they told a mountain to pick itself up and move, it would."[1]

Fellowship

A student minister reading this far might say, "I am fascinated and thrilled about focusing my student ministry on the glory of Christ. I can hardly wait to launch deeper discipleship, and I want to mobilize students to care for hurting people. I better ditch anything that looks like fun and games."

Throwing the proverbial baby out with the bath is a mistake. Fellowship only becomes a negative in student ministry when it gets out of balance and/or it is provided without purpose.

The body of Christ has embraced fellowship from the first hours of the Christian church. "They were continually devoting themselves to the apostles' teaching and to fellowship, to the breaking of bread and to prayer. . . . Day by day continuing with one mind in the temple, and breaking bread from house to house, they were taking their meals together with gladness and sincerity of heart, praising God and having favor with all the people" (Acts 2:42, 46–47). The Greek sometimes translated "breaking bread" can better be translated "shared a pizza and two sodas."

Christ turns strangers into family. "For through Him we both have our access in one Spirit to the Father. So then you are no longer strangers and aliens, but you are fellow citizens with the saints, and are of God's household" (Eph. 2:18–19).

"If we walk in the Light as He Himself is in the Light, we have fellowship with one another, and the blood of Jesus His Son cleanses us from all sin" (1 John 1:7).

Christ sacrificed His life, in part, so believers can experience joy together. "I came that they may have life, and have it abundantly" (John 10:10). Joy is a fruit of the Spirit (Gal. 5:22).

A few student ministers believe they can provide fun for teenagers *only* if it quickly leads to some noble purpose. Christ might reply that He delights in watching His kids find joy—period. On a slow day in heaven, maybe He swishes down a black diamond trail with one of His adopted teenagers. Maybe He gets a chuckle from the noises that only a cabin of middle-school boys can make after lights-out.

Fellowship and body life don't *have* to lead to some other purpose, but they may. The key is to define your target audience, define what you are trying to accomplish, and then carefully choose fellowship and recreation with the best potential for achieving that purpose.

Everyone knows quality fellowship experiences can deepen relationship bonds. But student ministers embracing a new paradigm will expand their thinking to consider building bonds:

- Among parents.

- Among students.

- Among volunteers.

- Between parents and volunteers.

- Between students and volunteers.

- Between students and their parents.

Christ absolutely adores His Father and enjoys a deep relationship with Him. That is what He wants His followers (including the teenage ones) to taste.

> "I do not ask on behalf of these alone, but for those also who believe in Me through their word; that *they may all be one*; even as You, Father, are in Me and I in You, that they also may be in Us, so that the world may believe that You sent Me. The glory which You have given Me I have given to them, that *they may be one*, just as We are one; I in them and You in Me, that they may be perfected *in unity*, so that the world may know that You sent Me, and loved them, even as You have loved Me" (John 17:20–23, emphasis added).

Chapter Eight
Evangelism, Ministry, and Missions

Evangelism, ministry, and missions are (or should be) inseparable. A cup of cool water given in the name of Christ leads to interest in who Christ is. A compassionate heart for evangelism should include a deep interest in the total person. Missions is ministry and evangelism both close at hand and far away. They are three . . . and one.

Evangelism

Writer/speaker Kevin Kirkland served as a youth pastor. Out of the blue, he once asked his wife, "Kimberly, when was the last time you remember seeing me brokenhearted over one of our students? I mean when was the last time you saw me just weep over someone who is lost or hurting?" Rather absent-mindedly she answered, "I don't know Kev—I would have to think about it."[1]

Kevin could not think of a single moment of brokenness in the recent past. That same afternoon he began a deep study of 2 Corinthians 5:14, across many translations. "For the love of Christ controls us" (NASV) or "compels us" (NKJV). Kevin declared his love for Christ and asked the Son of God to make him "lovesick" toward teenagers who are spiritual orphans. This led Kevin into a journey toward brokenness and concern for such students that now permeates his life and writings.

You

Student minister, what most motivates you to put in a hard day's work? To look successful and effective to the pastor and key church leaders? To look successful to those who set salary raises? To look cool to students?

To please Christ and to bring Him glory? What most motivates you will determine what you choose to do each day.

What are you passionate about? What do you go to sleep dreaming about in student ministry? What do you enjoy creating in your mind while you drive your car? Is it slightly possible that, as with the church in Laodicea, you have lost your first love? When you started out in student ministry, did the love of Christ compel you to introduce teenagers to Him, but now has putting posteriors in chairs become your life?

Evangelism is the intersection of brokenness for students and a hunger to glorify the Lord. "All creation is 'window dressing' for Christ's excellence. It all points to Him. . . . More amazing is the fact that God, Who was clothed with majesty, chose to become the personification of majesty when He came to earth in the form of His Son, Jesus Christ."[2] Paul wrote, "God was in Christ reconciling the world to Himself" (2 Cor. 5:19).

Your own awakening to God's Son leads naturally to a heart passion to see students and their families awakened as well. For those who do not have a relationship with Him, evangelism is the first step toward that full awakening.

Your Student Ministry

Forget the word *send*. You cannot send students and leaders to share their faith. You can only lead them.

A student ministry will not drift toward evangelism. It may drift in lots of other directions, but it won't drift toward a priority on evangelism. Guiding students to Christ will become a core value only because you have provided genuine, dramatic leadership in that direction.

When you champion the call to evangelism to students and leaders awakened to Christ, they will respond. Greg Stier reports: "As I travel the nation, I encounter teenagers everywhere who are sick and tired of typical church and dying instead for authentic Christianity. . . . They want a driving cause to live for and, if necessary, to die for. . . . The call of Christianity offers them all this and more. They must be energized, equipped, and turned loose with the life-changing, culture-transforming, world-shaking message of the gospel of Jesus Christ."[3]

There's a world of difference between saying,

God loves you and has a wonderful plan for your life,

and saying,

God has a wonderful plan for the nations, to sum up everything in heaven and earth under Jesus as Lord, and He loves you enough to give you a strategic place in it.

If you tell a skater God loves him and can make him a little happier, he may reply that it's simpler just to smoke something that will make him a little happier. It is an entirely different thing to tell him the God of the entire universe loves him so much that He is inviting him to join His Son in a lifetime of amazing kingdom adventures.

If you promote "benefits" when you call teenagers to salvation, you will get shallow believers with a little Jesus in their pocket. They will spend their lives valuing Jesus for those benefits He brings to them. But if you present the overwhelming majesty of the Son of God and the thrill of abandoning all to join in His kingdom adventures, those coming into His family will tend to wrap their entire lives around that challenge.

The Presence of the King

Awakening Christian students and the church to the supremacy of Christ offers the best hope for winning this generation of teenagers to Christ. All other programs and motivations eventually fall short.

The night before the Battle of Agincourt, the British soldiers were sick and tired and outnumbered four to one by the French army. The battle appeared unwinnable. Late in the night a hooded figure began to make his way through the British ranks, encouraging and challenging the soldiers. After a while the soldiers discovered who the visitor was— Edward IV, the king himself. The next day the larger, healthier French army was routed by the British. What made the difference? *The presence of the king.*

Ron Hutchcraft, who tells the story above, adds these words:

As people who can see the battle raging for a generation of young people, we look out at a scene that appears overwhelming. The enemy is bombarding kids with media and money we cannot begin to match. . . . Worst of all, the army of those who are willing to fight for young people are so small compared to the number of kids to reach and forces of darkness. On the eve of battle, we seem to be so outnumbered, so outgunned.

Except for the One who is walking among us, His troops. It is the *King Himself*—King Jesus, King of kings and Lord of lords. This is *His* battle to win. The decisive difference in this battle for the young people in our community is *the presence of the King in the midst of His army.*[4]

Ministry

Unless something happens, your teenagers will grow up to become just like the majority of American churchgoers. They:

1. Believe Christ exists primarily to do good things for them.
2. Believe being a "Christian" will help them achieve "the American dream."
3. Consider their luxuries and comforts to be benefits of their faith.
4. Love themselves more than they love others.
5. Construct flimsy arguments about the poor so they can excuse themselves from helping.
6. Give money to the church and to various ministries, as long as it does not affect their standard of living.
7. Are unlikely to express love to those who cannot return that love.

To use the vocabulary of Revelation 3, they are lukewarm. But here is a key question, Are they lukewarm *Christians*? In other words, will such church members make it to heaven? What does "spit you out of My mouth" (v. 16) sound like to you?

Prosperity has not been good for the American church. It never has been. "When I fed them, they were satisfied; when they were satisfied, they became proud; then they forgot me" (Hos. 13:6 NIV).

Read Matthew 25:37–40 slowly and carefully.

"Then the righteous will answer Him, 'Lord, when did we see You hungry, and feed You, or thirsty, and give You something to drink? And when did we see You a stranger, and invite You in, or naked, and clothe You? When did we see You sick, or in prison, and come to You?'"

(Don't miss Christ's remarkable answer.)

"The King will answer and say to them, 'Truly I say to you, to the extent that you did it to one of these brothers of Mine, even the least of them, you did it to Me.'"

"Jesus is saying that we show tangible love for God in how we care for the poor and those who are suffering. He expects us to treat the poor and the desperate as if they were Christ Himself. Ask yourself this: If you actually saw Jesus starving, what would you do for Him?"[5]

You might say to your students: "As we are feeding the group under the underpass, I want you to try to see each person as Jesus. Let the love and the respect you show be the same you would use toward Jesus in the flesh."

Fear and guilt are not the answer to motivation. God's Son wants students and families to love others extravagantly because they are overwhelmingly in love with Him. Galatians 5:13–14 notes, "For you were called to freedom, brethren; only do not turn your freedom into an opportunity for the flesh, but through love serve one another. For the whole Law is fulfilled in one word, in the statement, 'You shall love your neighbor as yourself.'"

It Begins with You

You pastor teenagers and their parents and volunteers. The flock will tend to follow the example of their shepherd.

Before you call others to sacrificial love and ministry, you must first inspect your heart. "Are you willing to say to God that He can have whatever He wants? Do you believe that wholehearted commitment to Him is more important than any other thing or person in your life? Do you know that nothing you do in this life will ever matter, unless it is about loving God and loving the people He made?"[6]

As you think carefully about your money and resources, maybe this should go on your refrigerator door:

> For Christ—Extravagance
> For those in need—Liberality
> For me—Simplicity

If you knew Christ were leading you to, would you move to a smaller house and give the proceeds from changing houses to poor people? Can you get as energized about downsizing possessions as getting something new? What is the most basic transportation that would allow you to meet your obligations?

A new way of thinking begins with you and then may permeate your student ministry. Picture a journey that would let you say . . .

I am moving away from tithes and offerings that require little change in my standard of living.	*I am moving toward* delighting in Jesus by giving so extravagantly that I must make major lifestyle adjustments.
I am moving away from concocting arguments that allow me to ignore the poor and those who are treated unjustly.	*I am moving toward* representing Christ in the lives of those in need in ways that change their situations.
I am moving away from believing I am superior to other groups of people.	*I am moving toward* humility and showing honor and deference toward all people Christ has created.
I am moving away from believing my faith and "the American dream" are tied together.	*I am moving toward* downsizing and simplicity in order to free significant funds for kingdom activity, including funds for those in need.
I am moving away from loving only those who might return the favor.	*I am moving toward* loving those who hate me or have nothing to offer in return.
I am moving away from wanting to be seen as cool rather than speaking of Christ.	*I am moving toward* considering all things as loss for the sake of introducing others to Jesus.
I am moving away from pursuing every opportunity to make myself better known or more powerful.	*I am moving toward* taking assignments only from Christ, including those that have me serving in obscurity.
I am moving away from expecting others to serve me.	*I am moving toward* serving others as Jesus did on earth.

Mobilizing Students for a Cause (People, Actually)

When students minister to one person in the name of Christ, that matters. But sometimes Christ is honored when a leader mobilizes students to confront a broader wrong, a wrong that is systemically hurting people.

One paraphrase of Scripture reads this way:

> "Tell my people what's wrong with their lives,
> face my family Jacob with their sins!
> They're busy, busy, busy at worship,
> and love studying all about me.
> To all appearances they're a nation of right-living people—
> law-abiding, God-honoring.
> They ask me, 'What's the right thing to do?'
> and love having me on their side.

81

But they also complain,
    'Why do we fast and you don't look our way?
    Why do we humble ourselves and you don't even notice?'

"Well, here's why:

"The bottom line on your 'fast days' is profit.
You drive your employees much too hard.
You fast, but at the same time you bicker and fight.
    You fast, but you swing a mean fist.
The kind of fasting you do
    won't get your prayers off the ground.
Do you think this is the kind of fast day I'm after:
    a day to show off humility?
To put on a pious long face
    and parade around solemnly in black?
Do you call that fasting,
    a fast day that I, God, would like?

"This is the kind of fast day I'm after:
    to break the chains of injustice,
    get rid of exploitation in the workplace,
    free the oppressed,
    cancel debts.
What I'm interested in seeing you do is:
    sharing your food with the hungry,
    inviting the homeless poor into your homes,
    putting clothes on the shivering ill-clad,
    being available to your own families.
Do this and the lights will turn on,
    and your lives will turn around at once.
Your righteousness will pave your way.
    The God of glory will secure your passage.
Then when you pray, God will answer" (Isa. 58:1–9 *The Message*).

Is evangelism optional? Is discipleship optional? Is mobilizing God's people to confront injustice optional?

- Is it possible a secular club at the high school is doing more to confront wrong than the church youth group?
- Is it possible a single teenager in the community has mobilized more support for some cause than a church filled with teenagers, parents, and volunteers?
- Is it possible teenagers who visit the youth group are surprised they hear lots of announcements about entertainment but none about helping people?

Teenagers at church tend to be seriously underchallenged. That is sad because right now many students are primed and ready to do hard things, to take on grand challenges. And developmentally they have a heightened sense of justice/injustice that can be channeled in powerful ways.

Brothers Alex and Brett Harris have become spokespersons for such a generation. At age nineteen they wrote: "We're not rebelling against institutions or even against people. Our uprising is against a cultural mind-set that twists the purpose and potential of the teen years and threatens to cripple our generation. Our uprising won't be marked by mass riots and violence, but by millions of individual teens quietly choosing to turn the low expectations of our culture upside down."[7] Students who do not find that challenge at church will just find it somewhere else.

An awakening to Christ will lead His people to go out in His name to stand with those toward whom His heart is tender.

Missions

Missions is evangelism and ministry. Both here and there and to the uttermost parts of the earth. It flows from passion for His name and His renown and an insatiable thirst to see the multiplication of worshippers before His throne for all of eternity.

The population in the U.S. represents only 5 percent of the population of the world. Ninety-five percent of U.S. believers stay in the U.S. to minister with that 5 percent. Five percent of U.S. believers go to minister with 95 percent of the world's population, a population that mostly does not know Christ.

A student minister might ask, "Should I personally take the good news of Christ to the nations, and should I mobilize our students to do the same?" The correct answer, when translated from the Greek, is *Duh*.

J. Hudson Taylor noted, "It will not do to say that you have no special call to go to (the nations). With these facts before you and with the command of the Lord Jesus to go and preach the gospel to every creature, you need rather to ascertain whether you have a special call to stay at home."[8]

Nothing except the church's aversion to sacrifice can make the evangelization of the world in this generation an impossibility. The good news is an awakening to God's Son makes joyful sacrifice entirely reasonable.

So now I had discovered five levels of callings from God—a calling to be saved, a calling for Jesus to be Lord, a calling to ministry, a calling to home missions, and a calling to foreign missions. . . . Why are there so many levels of Christian calling in our contemporary Christian community? Where are they found in the biblical text? I have a strange suspicion that the nuances of these "callings" have less to do with theology and more to do with the condition of the church. Paul seemed to think there was only one calling. He writes to Timothy, "So do not be ashamed to testify about our Lord, or ashamed of me his prisoner. But join with me in suffering for the gospel, by the power of God, who has saved us and called us to a holy life— not because of anything we have done but because of his own purpose and grace" (2 Timothy 1:8–9). The scriptures seem to

84

simplify the process of calling. The one call is to lay your life at the feet of Jesus and to do whatever he asks.[9]

Short-Term Mission Trips

Short-term mission trips are valuable components of student ministry. Many people are affected by involvement in short-term mission—some positively and some negatively. Short-term mission participants include not merely those who go but also those who send (3 John 5–8) and those who receive (Matt. 10:40–42).

Short-term mission is not an isolated event but rather an integrated process over time affecting all participants. This process consists of prefield, on-field, and postfield stages.

An increasing number of missions organizations desire to pursue excellence and to strengthen their overall effectiveness worldwide. They do so not in a legalistic or rigid manner but in a redemptive manner by voluntarily adopting and committing to standards of excellence in short-term mission efforts. To date, about seventy organizations have adopted the following *U.S. Standards of Excellence in Short-Term Missions*:

1. *God-Centeredness*—An excellent short-term mission seeks first God's glory and his kingdom, and is expressed through our:
   - *Purpose*—Centering on God's glory and his ends throughout the entire STM process
   - *Lives*—Sound biblical doctrine, persistent prayer, and godliness in all thoughts, words, and deeds
   - *Methods*—Wise, biblical, and culturally appropriate methods which bear spiritual fruit

2. *Empowering Partnerships*—An excellent short-term mission establishes healthy, interdependent, ongoing relationships between sending and receiving partners, and is expressed by:
   - Primary focus on intended receptors
   - Plans which benefit all participants
   - Mutual trust and accountability

3. *Mutual Design*—An excellent short-term mission collaboratively plans each specific outreach for the benefit of all participants, and is expressed by:
   - On-field methods and activities aligned to long-term strategies of the partnership
   - Goer-guests' ability to implement their part of the plan
   - Host receivers' ability to implement their part of the plan

4. *Comprehensive Administration*—An excellent short-term mission exhibits integrity through reliable set-up and thorough administration for all participants, and is expressed by:
   - Truthfulness in promotion, finances, and reporting results
   - Appropriate risk management
   - Quality program delivery and support logistics

5. *Qualified Leadership*—An excellent short-term mission screens, trains, and develops capable leadership for all participants, and is expressed by:
   - *Character*—Spiritually mature servant leadership
   - *Skills*—Prepared, competent, organized, and accountable leadership
   - *Values*—Empowering and equipping leadership

6. *Appropriate Training*—An excellent short-term mission prepares and equips all participants for the mutually designed outreach, and is expressed by:
   - Biblical, appropriate, and timely training
   - Ongoing training and equipping (prefield, on-field, postfield)
   - Qualified trainers

7. *Thorough Follow-up*—An excellent short-term mission assures debriefing and appropriate follow-up for all participants, and is expressed by:
   - Comprehensive debriefing (prefield, on-field, postfield)
   - On-field reentry preparation
   - Postfield follow-up and evaluation

(For much more detail about each of the standards noted above, go to www.stmstandards.org.)

Passports

Every student minister needs a passport today. Just having one indicates a heart prepared to respond quickly to any international summons the King sends. Student ministers with passports are in the best position to challenge every student, parent, and volunteer to have passports as well. The multiplication of passports through a student ministry helps create a corporate sense of anticipation and expectation that kingdom adventures are coming.

A GAP Year Mission Adventure after High School

Every Christian student should go on short-term mission projects throughout adolescence and beyond. But at least once every student needs the life-altering and kingdom-expanding challenge of going to the front lines for a longer period.

Every church youth group should do mission projects together. But at least once every student needs to go without the group to do what God uniquely has called and gifted him or her to do. Envision it becoming normative in your church that almost every student serve full-time in domestic or international missions for a summer, semester, or year, around age eighteen or nineteen. A full discussion about such a trip is in chapter 14.

Closing

Mission leaders today talk about a church for every people and the gospel for every person. For Christ's sake believers must be about the business of setting up bases of operation around the globe so His hope-filled message can impact every culture.

Those who research missionary advances estimate six million new churches are currently needed among over two billion non-Christians for the nations to be effectively reached for Christ and their cultures transformed by His power. That might mean 600,000 young missions volunteers sent forth by the Holy Spirit from existing churches on every continent.

How could this be possible? Christians must reembrace the consummate vision of the Lord's glory. Anything less will prove incapable of sustaining world outreach at the level required to finish the task. If American student ministries experience a Christ awakening, they could play a pivotal role in this missions drama.

Focus on the teenagers and families in your church as you read this challenge given by Billy Graham:

Let us light a fire
of renewed faith
to proclaim the gospel of Jesus Christ
in the power of the Holy Spirit, to the ends of the earth.
Using every resource at our command
and with every ounce of our strength.
Let us light a fire in this generation
that, by God's grace, will never be put out.
Let us light a fire
that will guide men and women into tomorrow and eternity.
Let the Light of the World shine through the whole earth
until He comes again.[10]

Chapter Nine
Discipleship

Student ministry volunteers impact the lives of students through many roles. This chapter gives primary attention to two of those roles—leading open groups and discipling students in one-on-three relationships.

These two roles are valuable but secondary to the home. Ideally, parents do not just reinforce teaching done by church leaders. Church leaders reinforce teaching done by parents. Parents do not just add their voices to the voices of those who are discipling their children. Disciplers add their voices in support of parents. But that being said, discipling at church still is vital kingdom activity.

Open-Group Bible Study

Churches have many different names for their primary Bible-teaching strategy for students—Sunday School, small-group Bible study, etc. This book uses the term *open groups* to apply to all those approaches. The name comes from the fact that the groups are always open to any student who shows interest in attending.

Open groups are valuable in student ministry.

- They frequently present how students can begin a relationship with Jesus.

- They teach new believers foundational concepts of discipleship.

- They present the plumb bob of God's Word to the largest number of students.

- They spiritually deepen students in preparation for one-on-three discipling.

- They assist new students with building a sense of belonging and community.

- They introduce students to adults who care for them and who are alive for Christ.

- They provide a positive experience for students whose families visit the church.

This book uses the term *small-group leader* to refer to those who lead open groups. Every teenager needs a small-group leader who is living out and communicating truth, who is inviting teenagers into deep prayer, and who is providing care and ministry. The life and teachings of this leader amplify and reinforce the voices of parents and others who disciple teenagers in one-on-three relationships.

For students not involved in one-on-three discipling, the small-group leader is the one member of the body of Christ (other than parents) most deeply committed to the spiritual well-being of the teenager. Because adults must balance many life responsibilities, most are not able to become involved life-on-life with more than about three students. Small-group leaders love all their members but are able to invest life-on-life with only a few of their students—those not involved in one-on-three discipling.

Open groups are a *vital* part of the new paradigm of student ministry. Churches not offering Bible study to all students should consider adding open groups. Churches who have boring open groups should give concerted attention to waking up those groups to Christ and to creating stimulating group sessions. They should provide the best curriculum available. They should budget to provide quality training for leaders. They should include open groups in advertising, communicating to students and parents the high value of this student ministry strategy.

True Bible Study

To be life-altering, open groups must offer true study of God's Word. That seldom is the case. Barry Shafer interviewed paid and volunteer youth leaders from twenty-seven churches in a metro area about their Bible studies. Roughly 70 percent said they offer some form of small-group Bible study. Then he asked them to describe the content of their studies using the following options:

1. Discussion of issues

2. Devotional talk by the leader

3. Bible reading and discussion

4. In-depth Bible study

None of the leaders described their teaching time as in-depth Bible study. When asked about their preparation for teaching, some answered, "I wing it."[1] Ouch.

Scott Duvall and Daniel Hays note:

How many times have I just "winged" it?

> While often unconscious of their interpretive method, many Christians today nonetheless frequently employ an *intuitive* or *feels-right approach* to interpretation. If the text looks as if it could be applied directly, then they attempt to apply it directly. If not, then they take a *spiritualizing approach* to the meaning—an approach that borders on allegorizing the biblical text (which shows little or no sensitivity to the biblical context). Or else they shrug their shoulders and move onto another passage, ignoring the meaning of the text altogether.[2]

What was missing in those student ministries above was inductive Bible study, or exegesis. Shafer notes that the three components of inductive study—observe, interpret, and apply—become three requests of God: "God, show me! God, teach me! God, change me."[3]

Any adult who teaches teenagers the Bible needs the same goal for them that Paul had for Timothy: "You, however, continue in the things you have learned and become convinced of, knowing from whom you have learned them, and that from childhood you have known the sacred writings which are able to give you the wisdom that leads to salvation through faith which is in Christ Jesus. All Scripture is inspired by God and profitable for teaching, for reproof, for correction, for training in righteousness; so that the man of God may be adequate, equipped for every good work" (2 Tim. 3:14–17).

Small-group Bible study that leads to new awakenings to Christ and to spiritual transformation can never, ever "just wing it." Too much is at stake. "For the word of God is living and active and sharper than any two-edged sword, and piercing as far as the division of soul and spirit, of both joints and marrow, and able to judge the thoughts and intentions of the heart" (Heb. 4:12).

As student minister, you equip the saints so they can lead true study of God's Word. To the best of your ability, you become "seminary" for those you lead, training them to use approaches and resources that lead to accurate interpretation.

One way you equip adults for Bible teaching is to model great Bible teaching/preaching when you are before the students. It is not your role to say what you think might be helpful to students but to proclaim and exposit what God already has said in Scripture. You teach the text, and then you draw application directly from that text. Topical studies that add "proof texts" to a human outline always will be full of shortfalls. On the other hand, great Bible teaching/preaching leads students directly to the Messiah.

One-on-Three Discipleship

The compliment to open groups is discipling relationships that involve more commitment and deeper relationships. The model presented in this chapter focuses on one adult and three students in a discipling relationship lasting at least one school year. This adult might be called a discipler, mentor, or even life coach. This discipling model mirrors the investment Jesus made in Peter, James, and John.

What one-on-three disciplers are doing is biblical and effective, growing disciples through relationships and while sharing life. They are following the example of Paul who reported, "We loved you so much that we were delighted to share with you not only the gospel of God but our lives as well, because you had become so dear to us" (1 Thess. 2:8 NIV).

Complementary but Different Strategies

Strangely, most churches provide two *open-group* gatherings as their only two discipling opportunities. For example, some churches provide open Bible study groups on Sunday mornings and topical study groups on Sunday evening or Wednesdays. Anyone may attend either set of groups with limited commitment. Both options may offer adult-student ratios of one-to-eight or even one-to-fifteen. Leaders on Sunday morning are not really engaged life-on-life with each student, nor are the leaders of topical studies.

Other churches offer open Bible study groups on church property and later offer open groups in homes. But again, the adult-to-student ratio still ranges around one-to-seven. The home atmosphere may be more relaxed, but that is not the same as an adult and a student experiencing life together and engaging in deep conversations about the faith.

Churches who offer two open groups must ask themselves this central question: After a year in two open groups (with limited life-on-life investment and interaction), are we seeing most students increasingly embracing the full supremacy of the Son, responding to His majesty in all of life, and inviting Him to live out His life through them? If the answer is no, then choosing a discipling option beyond open groups may make sense.

Open group discipleship and one-on-three discipleship are different, but they complement each other.

- Rather than open and fluid participation in open groups, students receive a one-on-three discipler only by making a covenant with that leader and with the others being discipled for a specific period of time.

- Rather than the foundational discipleship of open groups, one-on-three discipling is built around deeper concepts and spiritual disciplines.

93

- Rather than open-group teaching about how to meet Christ, one-on-three discipling presupposes students know Christ and now want to become conformed to His image.

- Rather than most study being done during the meeting times of open groups, students being discipled usually are accountable for preparation and spiritual disciplines outside of meeting times.

Relationships

The goal of student ministry is students who, for the glory of the Father and in the power of the Spirit, spend a lifetime embracing the full supremacy (supreme power and authority) of the Son, responding to His majesty in all of life, inviting Christ to live His life through them, and joining Him in making disciples among all peoples.

Adults called to disciple students may see that goal as almost overwhelming. It might cause some to ask, "To reach that goal, what is the most important thing I should do?" Actually, the most important thing is not what the adults should *do* but what he or she should *be*.

Nothing is more important to discipling students than the fact that *the discipler* embraces the supremacy of the Son, responds to His majesty in all of life, and joins Him in making disciples among all peoples. If the discipler increasingly is being transformed spiritually, has heart connections with those they disciple, and shares life with them in accountable relationships, then it is probable they increasingly will be alive to Christ.

Adults serving as an intentional spiritual shepherd to three teenagers
is costly in terms of time.
That is why such discipling is rare today.
Most churches have taken the easier route
and have tried to disciple students through programs.
One look at how many students fall away after high school
suggests the program approach has not worked.

The fact of the matter is, God Himself hardwired human beings for relationships. It should come as no surprise that He ordained most discipling would take place in the context of low-ratio relationships. Spiritual transformation is as much caught as taught, especially where teenagers are concerned.

Three Students

Students ready to move to the next level of their spiritual transformation need to be discipled in the context of a warm, safe, and vibrant relationship with a spiritually alive believer. Leaders "pastoring" a flock of three students might be ideal for several reasons.

1. *Span of Relationships*—Given the pace of life today, leaders may not have adequate discretionary time to share life with more than three students. It takes time to share a coffee, attend a recital, or swing by someone's work.

2. *Chaos and Pain*—Students often live lives marked by chaos and pain. It is important that students have a time and place to express what presently is making life hard. When they express those challenges, they need to hear from a compassionate leader and from compassionate peers who know them well. Finally, they need prayer from those close by. It takes time for a student to express a concern, hear compassionate and biblically sound responses, and receive targeted prayer. Multiplying that time by more than three may leave no time for other discipling activity.

3. *Articulating the Faith*—Discipled people need to be able to express their faith and beliefs in articulate ways. The discipling process must give them multiple opportunities to put their newfound learning into their own words. If they should do this poorly, they need feedback and then an opportunity to try again. Leaders with more than three disciples may discover too few minutes for such careful listening and teaching.

Leaders whose only discipleship approach is speaking to a large group of students receive almost no feedback related to learning or issues of the heart and will. They have almost no opportunity to hear from learners whether they are internalizing change and transformation. In essence, they throw a handful of the yeast of truth on the crowd. Those who disciple three students kneed and massage the yeast of truth into the dough of their lives.

1. *Awkwardness*—Some students would be entirely comfortable meeting one-on-one with an adult for a school year. Many would find that awkward. In addition, some parents would be a little uncomfortable having their teenager alone with one adult for so many hours.

    One of three students will be absent a fair number of times. Illness and circumstances outside a student's control are part of life. Absences do not create awkwardness when two other students still are available to meet with a leader.

    With the exception of parents who disciple their own children, adults disciple students of their gender. Discipling is different from teaching a class or leading a group. Disciplers need to engage in accountability discussions that might touch on sexual issues. Disciplers may need to provide transportation for students, meet them for coffee, connect at school activities, or visit in their homes. This degree of closeness between an adult and students suggests same-gender relationships.

2. *Linking the Teenager to Other Adults*—Leaders can assist in tying students to more adults in the congregation and even to more teenage peers. This process takes time. Trying to disciple too many students means fewer minutes are available to help each student build relationships with the full church.

3. *Bonding with Parents*—Wise disciplers care about the total lives of students and express that by building supportive relationships with students' parents and families. The time required to pursue those relationships with more than three students may be impractical.

Jesus discipled twelve, but He had twenty-four hours a day, seven days a week to build into those apostles. The group ate their meals together, and they lodged together. Three disciples may be more realistic for nondivine adults who do not live with students, who have other vocations, and who must care for their own families. As noted before, those three disciples can parallel the additional time and attention Jesus invested in Peter, James, and John.

Veteran discipler Greg Ogden concludes, "My conviction is that the primary way people grow into self-initiating, reproducing, fully devoted followers of Jesus Christ is by being involved in highly accountable, relational, multiplying discipleship units of three or four."[4]

Parents as One-on-Three Disciplers

Consider these two challenges:

1. In a youth group of thirty, twenty students might be motivated to enter a one-on-three relationship. That would require about seven disciplers. In a youth group of three hundred, two hundred might want to be discipled, requiring seventy disciplers. The student minister of a small church might be just as discouraged about finding seven disciplers as a large-church student minister trying to enlist seventy. Where will all those adults come from? (It may not be obvious at the beginning, but Christ's provision always is adequate, even extravagant).

2. Parents today have almost no memories of being discipled by their parents (or anyone else). And few have been challenged or trained to disciple their children.
   Inertia is the tendency of a body at rest to remain at rest. Overcoming inertia requires great effort. Home-discipling inertia is the tendency of parents who always have left discipling to the church to continue to do so. On the front end, parents will need a specific strategy to begin intentionally discipling their students for the first time on an ongoing basis.

Challenging, enlisting, and equipping parents to be one-on-three disciplers can be a solution to both dilemmas. First, enlisting a fair percentage of Christian parents to disciple may be the only way to get ratios down to one to three.

Second, leading parents to commit to a day and time to disciple their children (and two friends of their children) may lead to more consistency than discipling at home.

> Granted, Deuteronomy 6:7 calls parents to disciple when they "sit in their house."
> That has to be the long-term goal. But for now it may take parents' discipling at church to overcome initial inertia.

Families tend to live with chaotic schedules and many pressures. Parents challenged to disciple at home may start off with the best of intentions. But in the real world they tend to fall back into old routines (and no discipling) after just a few weeks.

Even if, temporarily, parents primarily disciple their children at church, they still can spiritually lead at home. As chapter 12 makes clear, Deuteronomy 6 parents make the beginning and ending of the day spiritually meaningful, and they model and teach truth "as they walk in the way." For now, rich discipling experiences at church may accelerate families adopting similar faith conversations at home.

Many students at church have parents who have not yet met Christ in a personal way. Others have parents who are such shallow believers they are not prepared to provide spiritual leadership for their teenagers. One-on-three discipleship is still possible for those students. Spiritually alive parents can disciple their own teenager and two of his or her friends whose parents are not involved.

Initially parents may have some motivation to disciple their own children but less motivation to disciple others. You and other church leaders must give them vision that leads to motivation. You need to say that they are changing the world. You might build on themes similar to these:

1. Do you desire to leave a legacy once you have gone to glory? Knowing that those you discipled are now taking Christ to a third generation can be a valuable legacy.

2. Are things happening in our country and world that concern you? Do you choose to curse the darkness or light a candle? Those you disciple can be part of building a better world for the glory of Christ.

3. Do you want the friends who most impact your child to have a shallow or a deep faith? Could three you disciple become a cord of three strands, ready to stand strong in a culture in crisis?

For parents too spiritually shallow to disciple students, lead teams provide a comfortable place to plug into student ministry. In addition to their service, such parents get to share time with other parents and teenagers who may be an inspiration to them. Parents who grow spiritually while serving on teams may well become ready to disciple three students.

Even during the turbulence of adolescence, the words of parents are powerful. Students fortunate enough to be discipled by their parents will experience special benefits.

Begin and Build

Few churches about to begin one-on-three discipling will sense they have an adequate number of disciplers. Feeling overwhelmed with the ideal number of disciplers needed accomplishes little.

It is better to begin with a limited number of disciplers than to do nothing until more appear.

Once underway, church leaders and disciplers should give continuing attention to discovering and calling out more parents and adults who can become disciplers. Student ministers who have three disciplers and need seven call out the others one at a time. Student ministers who have forty and need seventy do the same thing. The key is to begin courageously and then take one step at a time.

Flexibility

The expression *one-on-three* is just a general way to view a discipling process. In the real world, discipling by parents may take place in slightly different ways.

1. A father and mother may have only one child, but both may want to be disciplers. Dad may disciple the son and two of his friends, while the mother disciples three girls not related to her.

2. A father and mother may only have one child, and both may want to disciple just their son.

3. A single mother may have one son. For now, she may want him to be discipled by a godly man while she disciples three girls. Or she may want to disciple her son alone.

4. A single dad may have one son, but because of the tension in their relationship just now, he may want the son to be discipled by someone else while the dad disciples three boys.

Parents, rather than church leaders, usually best understand the nuances of home relationships and can best decide how to form one-on-three groupings.

The Discipling Process

Life Coaches

Parents and others who lead one-on-three discipleship can be called disciplers, mentors, or even life coaches. In general, a life coach is an advisor who helps people with problems, decisions, and goal attainment in daily life.

Parents in the business world increasingly are exposed to the practice of life coaching. Using this term at church may help them understand quickly what role they can play with a teenager.

In addition, many parents have coached their children in sports teams over the years. Using the title *life coach* may help some to see discipling as a new way to coach teenagers in the game of life.

The term *coach* or *discipler* might suggest that spiritual impact is moving in only one direction. Actually, all genuine discipleship is reciprocal. Adults on their own journey toward transformation will always be watching for ways their young disciples can speak truth to them, pray over them, and model Christ's life before them.

Some student ministries may be blessed with many parents who already are spiritually transformed and who handle Scripture well. In such a setting life coaches can both present biblical truth to their three students and then coach students as they apply that truth to life.

Some student ministries today may not have a large majority of parents who are ready to handle Scripture well. As a transition strategy, student ministers may need to present biblical content to teenagers while inviting and equipping parents to coach those teenagers toward biblical life application. The student minister might present biblical truth to all students and leaders for about fifteen minutes, followed by thirty minutes of coaching in one-on-three groupings.

Life coaches (or mentors or disciplers if those titles are used) can begin their coaching time by asking: Can you tell me, in your own words, the heart of the biblical message you just heard from the student minister? (Learners who cannot accurately communicate truth in their own words have not truly learned.)

After clarifying truth, the coach then can divide the remaining time among the three students. In some settings this might allow ten minutes of focus on each student. For those ten minutes, the coach might lead each student through this process.

1. Based on the biblical truth you have heard and something happening in your life, where are you most interested or troubled?

2. More specifically, where are you today with that situation?

3. Way down the road, how might Christ use this situation for His glory and bring His kingdom on earth?

4. As Christ lives out His life through you, what are some different ways that may look in this situation? (Remember Christ's life is more being than doing.)

5. Which of these ways of moving forward appeal to you since it seems most like Him?

6. How do you need the three of us to pray for you as you move forward?

7. Last week you shared with us your desire to move forward on a particular issue. How did that go? Is Christ nudging you toward a course correction as you continue to move forward?

Of course, this is just the part of discipling that takes place at a particular hour each week. Equally valuable is the discipling that takes place as the discipler and the disciple share life. Movies often are based on novels. The Bible is "the Book," and a discipler's life is "the movie" based on the Book. Watching the discipler live life allows the disciple to see biblical truth as visceral and real, both the being and the doing.

Wise disciplers often invite their three students into their home. Being a godly single, spouse, or parent in the presence of impressionable teenagers is powerful discipleship. Other rich venues for discipleship are the adult's workplace, the teenager's workplace, the teenager's extracurricular activities, and recreation conducive to conversation. Jesus certainly sat and taught some of the time, but mostly He discipled while sharing life with the apostles.

Major Student Ministry Gathering

The major student ministry gathering of the week (beyond Sunday morning) may look like this:

15 minutes   Body Life
Joyful experiences that celebrate and build relationships

30 minutes	Worship through Music
	Focused on the majesty of Christ
15 minutes	Proclamation of Biblical Truth
	Presented by the student minister
30 minutes	One-on-Three Life Coaching
	Ten minutes of focus on each student
15 minutes	Concerted Prayer in One-on-Three Groups
	Flowing out of worship, Scripture, and discipling

Schedules

Some student ministers may sidestep parents as life coaches because their involvement does not fit the weekly church schedule. Some might say, "The adults are in another meeting at that hour and are not available."

That is a clear example of the tail wagging the dog. First church leaders clarify mission. Then they choose programming and ministries to achieve the mission. *Then* they build a schedule around those mission-focused programs and ministries.

Biblical Discipling Content

The discipling curriculum or teaching approach must provide biblical content for meetings but also provide a process students use to dig for and discover biblical truth and insights between those meetings. Ideally the curriculum will prompt higher thought processes than filling in blanks.

The curriculum or teaching approach *must* include a focus on who Christ is today. Only students who increasingly are embracing the supremacy of Christ will embrace the spiritual disciplines. Only those students falling more and more in love with Jesus and in awe of His majesty will hunger for righteousness and morality in every area of life. Only students shifting their view of Christ from mascot to Monarch will place opportunities to go deeper in Him ahead of other calendar options. Only those adoring Him in entirely new ways will desire to be equipped for His kingdom adventures. The goal for every discipler/life coach should be:

To the best of my ability,
I have helped those I disciple to leave my presence
with a deeper understanding of the glory of Christ
and a fuller hope shaped by the supremacy of Christ.

Curriculum that provides simplistic answers to teen problems but never points them toward the King who is the Answer is best used for lining the bottom of parakeet cages. To see a Christ-focused curriculum specifically designed for one-on-three discipleship, go to www.oneonthree.com.

Making Disciples Who Make Disciples

Most churches will experience more advantages when adults are included in discipling students than when older students alone disciple younger students.

- Adults may have richer life experiences they can draw from as they present spiritual truth.

- Adults may have knowledge and experience that better equip them to respond to crisis issues that arise with their students, including life-threatening issues.

- Adults can link their students to other adults in the congregation, creating for each student a richer web of relationships.

- Adults can form bonds with parents, sometimes leading to ministry to the entire family.

But adult leadership must not lead to passive students. The goal of discipleship is not just making disciples. The goal is making disciples so enthralled with Jesus, so full of His aroma, and so expressive of His life that they make disciples. They become high school graduates who are motivated and equipped to disciples others in college, trade school, the military, the workplace, or the home. The discipler's goal is to serve as a multiplier, preparing the hearts of the students they disciple to reproduce themselves.

All three students need to feel engaged during discipling/coaching sessions. The two students not in focus during coaching need to be actively involved with the student who is. They need to ask perceptive questions. They need to share biblical truth and life experiences that can be helpful to the student who is in focus. Participating in the process should allow students increasingly to become skilled as disciplers/life coaches on their own.

- In middle-school groups the adult may take primary leadership while the teenagers support.
- In younger high school groups the adult and teenagers may share leadership.
- In older high-school groups the teenagers may do most of the coaching while the adult supports.

Giving students active roles has another advantage beyond building disciple-makers. Christ can work through students to bless adults. At times students may have more of the passion leaders somehow lost in adulthood. Or they may feel less fear in following orders from the King. Or they may have fresh insights into Scripture less tainted by church culture. Or they may have found ways to pray with more intimacy. As adults open the way for students to lead in discipleship, leaders can and will be blessed.

Equipping Disciplers

Student ministers equip disciplers/coaches before they begin discipling students. "The things which you have heard from me in the presence of many witnesses, entrust these to faithful men who will be able to teach others also" (2 Tim. 2:2). Attention should be given to the spiritual disciplines, the curriculum that will be used, group dynamics, understanding students, and intercessory prayer. This might take place during a late-summer leadership retreat. Or potential disciplers might meet weekly for a school semester before they are given their three students to disciple.

As a best practice a student minister (or someone the minister equips) should meet once a week with the disciplers after they begin meeting with students. The spiritual depth and vitality of the disciplers will be a key variable impacting the transformation of the students.

Disciplers must come to see this time as *their* primary discipleship experience through the church. They must see this time not as a *meeting* but as the gathering of a *community* that is valuable to them. They must believe serving is this ministry and attending such gatherings has added value to their lives. They should be willing to say they would give up many other things before they would give up discipling students and connecting with the student minister and the other disciplers.

Finding a weekly time for this meeting will be a challenge. Some churches will find success providing this meeting immediately before coaching/discipling begins—during the same time the teenagers are participating in body life and music worship. Student ministers who believe it is strategic to be with the disciplers can equip others to lead body life and music worship. Student ministers who believe it is strategic to lead body life and music worship can equip others to meet with the disciplers.

A session with the disciplers/coaches might include:

1. Celebration of spiritual victories.
2. Problem-solving related to issues/crises arising in the groups.
3. Examination of future teaching content.
4. Continuing training in how to build relationships and to disciple/coach.
5. Experiencing spiritual disciplines and accountability.
6. Intercessory prayer for the disciplers and the students.

Adults need to be full participants in the spiritual disciplines, including accountability. At times adults may need to report to their students that they have been completely accountable to adult peers but they are not sharing all the details with the students. Students may not have the maturity to handle hearing all the details of adult failures, but they do need to know leaders are modeling the same accountability they call students to experience.

The student minister should be a participant rather than an aloof leader in the discipleship process, modeling accountability and authenticity. Even more importantly, student ministers should speak openly about new ways they are waking up to the supreme majesty of Christ, new ways they are learning to adore Him, and new invitations He is making to student ministers to join Him in His kingdom activity. The student minister's awakening will be contagious.

Parent Disciplers and Heart Connections

As chapter 12 makes clear, warm relationships (heart connections) are the conduit that carry spiritual impact from parent to child. This is true at home, and it is true in discipling.

One of the highest priorities of any student ministry is building stronger and stronger heart connections between parents and students. Churches that do well with this will find teenagers and parents pleased with the idea of experiencing one-on-three discipleship together.

On the other hand, if teenagers and parents grumble about being together, they have simply given evidence that more attention needs to be given to heart connections. As relationships increasingly warm up, more and more families can be drawn into the discipling process. Chapter 12 provides concrete strategies for building heart connections.

Note: Open-group (Sunday School, small-group Bible study, etc.) leaders can be included in this meeting. They have the same need for spiritual growth and accountability. They have the same need to receive spiritual leadership from the student minister. One-on-three disciplers and small-group leaders can meet together for spiritual growth and then separate to focus on their unique curricula and approaches.

As a best practice, you also might consider meeting informally, one-on-one, with the disciplers at some other time each month or quarter.

- In this regard you are modeling what you want disciplers to do with their students.

- You are acknowledging that you cannot make the maximum impact on the discipler without having direct contact with that person's home, family, friends, and work.

You should include spouses or associates in meetings or activities with disciplers of the opposite sex.

As a best practice, you also might give a minimum of one hour per week to administrative issues related to disciplers/coaches.

- As with any organism, neglect will lead to dysfunction and eventually to death.

- The administration of discipling is a core function of student ministry. Student ministers perform that function with excellence before they give time to less important activities.

- Moving to a lead team strategy may allow you to spend much less time on future events. This opens up large blocks of time for initiating and strengthening discipleship.

Administrative Issues

Annual Schedule

Students and leaders make a commitment to one-on-three discipleship for at least a school year. With time off for holidays, such a schedule might call for about twenty-eight weeks of commitment. For consistency a curriculum that provides discipling content should be provided for those twenty-eight weeks. Students who make a commitment to discipling year after year will need fresh content each year.

Family vacations and church trips make weekly group meetings in the summer difficult. Both students and adults also may need a break from the intensity of group relationships. Having the summer off might allow both groups to approach the fall with renewed enthusiasm for forming new discipling relationships.

Leaders can challenge students to view summer and holidays as laboratory experiences. They can present missions and ministry events as a direct outgrowth of discipling experiences. Also, off weeks allow students to test whether they are becoming consistent with the spiritual disciplines even without weekly accountability. One-on-three disciplers can continue to show care for the lives of students through calls and electronic communications.

Calling Out Disciplers

Parents can be the primary disciplers of teenagers, but most churches will need to add other adults to get ratios down to one to three. Every adult in the congregation who is spiritually alive and emotionally healthy should be considered a potential discipler. Adults who may never become typical youth volunteers or sponsors can make a unique contribution by becoming disciplers to three students.

- Disciplers need a walk with Christ that is alive and growing.

- They need the capacity to offer unconditional love to students that is warm and safe.

- They need to comply with church policies related to background checks and waiting periods.

- They must have an identity grounded in who they are in Christ. There is no place for adults who want to have their needs met by students or by the status of being a leader.

Current disciplers may know of adults who have potential. With proper approval disciplers might invite an adult to serve as an apprentice with them. Over time such a plan might allow the church to launch many adults into full discipling relationships of their own.

Wise student ministers ask teenagers: "Who do you most respect spiritually? Who would you want to be discipled by?" In fact, teenagers can even make the first invitation to an adult to become a discipler (if the candidate meets the criteria noted above). Their fresh faces may be harder to say no to than a staff member.

The senior pastor and other spiritual leaders can create a culture that supports relational discipleship. Adults consistently should be led to discover their spiritual gifts, challenged to invest those gifts in others, and motivated to leave a legacy in the next generation through discipling.

Among the prospects for disciplers of students are:

- Parents of students willing to invest in other people's children.
- Adults who have been discipled and now are ready to invest in others.
- College students.
- Single adults.
- Members of men's ministries wanting to leave a legacy.
- Members of women's ministries wanting to invest in a relationship.
- Senior adults with warm hearts toward the young.

Transitions between Student Ministers

All the stakeholders in student ministry can agree to search for new student ministers who will commit to supporting the church's discipling approach. Too often students experience whiplash as a succession of student ministers launch their own approach to discipling. Students deserve consistency in discipling approaches across their teenage years.

Consistency

Most churches will discover it will take one or two years to see discipling functioning smoothly and producing visible fruit. Leaders who intend to build a long-term ministry will view that period as a reasonable investment.

One-on-three discipling is not a fad to be abandoned the first time a challenge arises. If some decide discipling "isn't working," the challenge is to identify the specific obstacle involved and then to work to remove it. Abandoning the approach is not the solution.

Relational discipleship is the approach Jesus used, and thus it transcends time and trends. It should become the standard in contemporary student ministry.

Relationship between One-on-Three Discipling and Open Groups

One-on-three discipleship and open-group Bible study (Sunday School, small-group Bible study, etc.) are complementary ministries.

- Students being discipled should see open groups as both a place where they can grow spiritually and an expression of their personal ministry.

- Students being discipled can see open groups as a strategy they can use in reaching friends and family for church attendance and an introduction to Christ.

- Students being discipled can sense a call to fulfill the purpose of fellowship by building warm relationships with all who attend open groups.

- Both open-group leaders and students being discipled consistently should seek to move open-group attendees into one-on-three discipling relationships.

Churches that do not provide one-on-three discipleship (or something similar) often create unrealistic expectations for open-group leaders. They hand those leaders a roster with twenty names and then say, "Please visit in *all* these homes and build relationships with the forty parents, and go by and visit *all* these students where they work, and attend their sporting events and concerts, and meet *all* twenty for coffee when they are in crisis, and celebrate their birthdays and accomplishments, and work your full-time job, and meet the needs of your own family, and cure cancer, and achieve world peace."

Disciplers *can* form heart connections with three students and share life with them. Most adults *cannot* invest in many more. That is why *both* open groups and one-on-three discipleship are vital.

Students genuinely discipled during their teenage years
are much more likely to
spend a lifetime
embracing the full supremacy of the Son,
responding to his majesty in all of life,
inviting Christ to live His life through them,
and joining Him in making disciples among all peoples.

What a return on this investment of life!

Chapter Ten
The Student Minister

This chapter might have caught your eye on the contents page, but this is a weak place to begin reading. This chapter and the new paradigm of student ministry that permeates this book only make sense after reading chapters 1 through 5. Please consider reading those chapters before returning here.

No Student Minister?

If your church has no student minister, one of the student ministry volunteers needs to fill some or all of the functions of a student minister. Should that be you? Even if student ministry is coordinated by a team, someone needs to chair the team. Someone needs to represent student ministry on churchwide planning teams and in calendar and budget planning. Someone needs to take the lead in writing and communicating a purpose statement and in strategic planning.

Whoever will take the lead role needs to read and digest this chapter. Almost all of it is as vital for an unpaid leader as for a vocational minister on staff.

The Student Minister (or Lead Volunteer)

Your awaking to the full supremacy of Jesus, your more deeply adoring Him on His throne, and your daily inviting Him to live His life through you . . . offers the brightest hope for your entire student ministry moving in those same directions. Your highest priority, both personally and vocationally, is to journey toward more fully embracing the full supremacy of His Son, increasingly thinking and acting as He does, and joining Him to make disciples for Him among all peoples.

Embracing that priority will change things.

- It will shape the content of your prayers.

- It will shape your worship before the throne.

- It will shape your attention to the spiritual disciplines.

- It will shape the books you read and the people with whom you pursue a relationship.

- It will shape your meditation on the Scriptures that present the supremacy of God's Son.

Doubling your student ministry budget does not have the same potential for impact as *your* awakening to more of all Christ is today. Your church's building a multimillion-dollar youth center does not have the same potential for impact as *your* awakening to more of all Christ is today. Are you on a journey in that direction?

From time to time you might return to the following questions just to help you detect growth:

- Are you discovering that extra sleep is not as appealing to you as early morning time standing before Christ enthroned?

- In the past two weeks or so, can you recall being in an informal conversation where you shared something you are discovering about Christ?

- When you speak of Christ with teenagers these days, do they detect in your face and voice a sense of wonder and delight?

- Can you recall giving a talk or teaching a lesson lately focused on how majestic King Jesus is *today*? (Sadly, most talks and lessons focus on self-help topics and hot-button issues rather than the One who is the source for all that teenagers need.)

- When you glance back at notes from your talks and lessons, do you see that you are more often using the names of Christ and less just "God" (when it is the Son you really intend to speak of)? (Increasingly the church Christ founded is using His names less and less.)

- Do you tend to use the phrase "Jesus is Lord" in a demanding and punitive way rather than allowing awakening and adoration to lead to a joyful embracing of the kingship of Christ?

- Deep inside yourself, can you detect that all you are discovering about Christ is causing hope to replace discouragement?

- Have you begun to feel that through the Spirit's power you are "infecting" others with an awakening to the supremacy of the Messiah?

Your Role

A few leaders say your church should terminate your role. They say the position of student minister no longer has relevance. They are both right and wrong.

The position of student minister may no longer have relevance when the student minister:

- Enjoys always being the center of attention and affection by students.

- Pushes parents away from student ministry (except when he needs funds or help).

- Responds to poor parenting only by trying to help students survive it.

- Sees volunteers as a workforce to make *his* program successful.

- Responds to poor teaching by volunteers by making himself the primary teacher.

- Brings *his* student ministry approach when he arrives and solely sets the calendar each year.

- Spends so much time preparing for major events that he can never address what should have been higher priorities.

You need feel no stress if some of those statements sound a bit like you. Those statements mostly typify how student ministry has been done the past sixty years. Only now is that approach being called into question. And it is very likely powerful people in your church fully expect you to follow some of the statements above. They may have called you to the church with such understandings, and they may be evaluating you today the same way.

But what if church leaders start discovering which factors really do lead to a sustainable faith among students? What if they begin to abandon thinking reflected by the statements above? What if they begin to envision church life for students very different from patterns of the past? What if they embrace the new way of thinking summarized in this book? Should the church then declare your job has no relevance and terminate you?

Absolutely not.

Every surgeon used to cut people with knives. No one knew any better. Then someone figured out a laser could cut tissue more precisely and with less bleeding. When news of lasers began to spread, did the medical community fire all the surgeons? Of course not.

Surgeons quickly begin to attend classroom and hands-on training in laser procedures. As soon as they were skilled with the new techniques, they began performing all appropriate surgeries that way.

A student minister who does not know how to partner with parents is no different from a surgeon who did not know how to hold a laser tool. A student minister who aggressively pursues training in parenting issues is no different from a surgeon who went to laser seminars. A student minister who becomes competent in partnering with parents is no different from the surgeon who now performs laser surgeries all day long. (Well, except for about $150,000 difference in salary).

Student ministers who hold tenaciously to patterns of the past may be a dying breed. But student ministers who embrace and become competent with new paradigms of ministry will be valuable to churches all their lives.

A New Paradigm for Student Ministry

Chapter 5 presented a new way of looking at student ministry. Here are some of the major concepts.

- Every goal for student ministry begins with a focus on the supremacy of Christ.
- Students are most likely to embrace the supremacy of Christ when they have heart connections with significant adults in their lives who increasingly embrace the supremacy of Christ.

Therefore:

- Student ministers must partner with pastors and teachers, in the power of the Spirit, to lead adults who are significant to students increasingly to embrace the supremacy of God's Son.
- Student ministers must partner with pastors and teachers, in the power of the Spirit, to lead students and the significant adults in their lives to build heart connections with each other.
- Student ministers must partner with parents and volunteers to lead students to build heart connections with peers.
- Student ministers must guide planning teams in designing programming that allows students and *the significant adults in their lives* to embrace and live out the supremacy of Christ together some of the time.
- Student ministers must guide planning teams in designing programming that allows students to embrace and live out the supremacy of Christ with *peers* some of the time.
- Student ministers must teach and live out biblical truth before students in ways that reinforce the impact of significant adults in students' lives.

Time

Student ministers already approaching burnout from their workload may reasonably ask how they will find the minutes to move in such dramatically new directions. The only reasonable answer seems to be to stop spending so much time preparing for major events and projects. Just as Jethro instructed Moses (Exod. 18:17–23), you need to empower God's people to do what they can do so you have time to do what only you can do.

If you get out of the event management business, you suddenly will discover you have *many* hours in the week to commit to higher priorities. Lead teams can make this happen.

Lead teams serve to implement events or projects calendared by the core planning team. Examples include a retreat, an all-night prayer gathering, or a family remodeling project at the rescue mission. Teams do not do all the work on events and projects. They may involve many members in their work. They simply take the lead, coordinating role.

Lead teams are effective in hundreds of churches. Chapter 6 has all the details. For now accept by faith that implementing lead teams opens the door to coordinating a new paradigm in student ministry *and* having a balanced life.

The Church Moving to the New Paradigm

Challenges abound if a church tries to adopt *only parts* of the new paradigm.

- If you try to move into new arenas of ministry but you also keep managing all student ministry events yourself, you will burn out.

- If the church moves to lead teams and you do not move into new arenas of ministry, you will be seen as lazy.

- If the church shifts their thinking about student ministry but you don't, you will get poor evaluations of your work, and you might be terminated.

- If you create a discipling ministry but those who preach and teach adults never call them to those ministries, you will have to tell most students you have no one to disciple them.

- If you decide to train parents to be spiritual leaders but they do not know that is their biblical role, you will train lots of empty chairs.

- If parents decide they should be their children's most important spiritual leaders but church leaders do not show them how, they will be frustrated.

- If the congregation decides building strong bonds with students is valuable but all of your programming keeps students isolated, they will question your leadership.

- If you decide building heart connections between members of the congregation and students is valuable but no one leads the adults in that direction, you will promise students new relationships that never will materialize.

Accelerating Coordinated Change

The naval armada of student ministry in your church needs to turn all at one time, or ships are going to start crashing into one another. Ideally, all the stakeholders in student ministry need to link arms to pray, study, and discuss the possibility of making major shifts in the church's ministry with students and families. Then, as they sense Christ's leadership, they need to make those changes *together*.

Leading many vocational ministers, volunteers, parents, and leaders in the congregation to read this book may dramatically accelerate change. Your reading the book alone is like lighting a little kindling next to logs soaked in water. Your getting many to read the book is like lighting a little kindling next to logs soaked with kerosene.

Changes That May be Coming

Appendix E: Forty Days toward Change presents a plan for leading your church toward change. During forty days it is possible the following changes will occur.

Parents may come to believe:

- Their awaking to the supremacy of Jesus, more deeply adoring Him on His throne, and daily arising to join Him in His kingdom activity offers the brightest hope for their children moving in those same directions.

- Communicating with Christ through prayer must permeate their homes and all of student ministry.

- They are to be the most important spiritual leaders to their children.

- They need instruction in that role, and they value those who provide it.

- They want to build and maintain heart connections with their children to maximize their spiritual influence.

- They need instruction in parenting approaches most likely to lead to heart connections with their children, and they value those who provide it.

- They value their children's building close relationships with members of the congregation.

- They feel called to join lead teams to express their ministry gifts and to give you time for your higher priorities.

Members of the congregation may come to believe:

- Their awakening to the supremacy of Jesus, more deeply adoring Him on His throne, and daily arising to join Him in His kingdom activity offers the brightest hope for the students of the church moving in those same directions.

- Communicating with Christ through prayer must permeate the church, including student ministry.

- They want to contribute to a grace-filled, welcoming church atmosphere that causes students to feel valued.

- They want to build heart connections with students, especially their prayer partners, to maximize their spiritual influence.

- They recognize parents should be the primary spiritual leaders to their children, and they support them in that role.

The remainder of this chapter will assume *most* (let's be realistic) of the stakeholders in student ministry have made a decision to move toward a new paradigm in student ministry.

Parents, Volunteers, and the Congregation

Your primary calling is not to disciple personally every student in your ministry. Your primary calling is to call out and equip the two groups of people that have the greatest potential for developing students who look like Jesus—the parents and caring members of the body of Christ. Student ministry pacesetter Mark DeVries notes, "I realize my primary work (as a youth worker) is to be an architect, helping to build a constellation of relationships with Christ-like adults for every teenager in my program."[1]

Parents
Training in Parenting—You may be twenty-two and single. You may be forty, rearing your own teenagers, and have a Ph.D. in family life education. In either case you can be a valuable partner with parents in rearing their teenagers.

If you are an expert in family life, you can train parents in parenting and in spiritual leadership yourself. If you are not a content expert, you can take the lead in getting those who are in front of your parents.

Regardless of your age, family situation, or degrees, you can:

- Tell parents you consider them the most important spiritual leaders in the lives of their children.

- Extend warm friendship to parents every time you cross paths with them.

- Partner with other church leaders to awaken parents further to the supremacy of Christ.

- Share the good news of Christ with parents who do not know Him.

- Ensure church leaders focused on adults join you in sharing the good news of Christ with every parent who does not know Him.

- Join parents in genuine prayer when their families are in crisis.

- Honor parents in every public and private conversation you have with students.

- Budget (or ensure other church leaders budget) to provide instruction in parenting and spiritual leadership in the home.

- Balance the student ministry calendar so it does not create schedule stress in homes and overly separate families.

- Guide the core planning team to plan a balance of programming that brings parents and students together.

Parents Outside the Church—Student ministers sometimes say, "An expanded ministry to parents and families in my church is impractical since over half my active students have parents who do not know Christ." That is similar to saying, "We have some divorced people in our church so we have given up talking about God's call to lifetime marriages." Or, "Eighty percent of our active members do not tithe so we have given up on any call to stewardship." Just abdicating to the culture cannot be the solution.

Rather than hand-wringing over the absence of parents in the church, the better plan might be to go reach them.

- Keep a running list of the names and addresses of unreached parents.
- Continually share names with church leaders who focus on introducing adults to Christ.
- Continually watch for opportunities to build relationships and share the gospel with parents yourself.
- Teach students how their lives and words can lead parents toward Jesus.

Preparing Parents to Disciple—How much does your church spend on *God's Plan B* for discipleship and spiritual transformation? In other words, how much does your church spend preparing to teach the Bible on church property? What are you investing in printed resources, bringing in trainers for your teachers, building educational buildings, and providing teaching supplies?

How much does your church spend on *God's Plan A* for discipleship and spiritual transformation? In other words, what budget funds do you invest to prepare parents to teach the Bible to their own children or to prepare some parents to lead their children to Christ? How many times this past year have church leaders gathered parents to inspire and train them to teach the things of God to their children?

As you read chapter 12, you will see recommendations that will require budget support. You and other church leaders will have to decide if Plan A really is going to be supported as the highest priority.

The Future—Strong leaders can picture the future before others do. If you develop a clear vision of an expanded ministry to and with parents and families, your church likely will follow. Pause right now to picture what the future may hold.

1. Envision God's being pleased the church is respecting His biblical principles regarding the roles of parents and families.

2. Envision that Christian parents will again turn their hearts toward their children, including their teenage children (Mal. 4:6; Luke 1:17).

3. Envision that Christian teenagers, because of new warmth and intimacy flowing from their parents, will again turn their hearts toward those parents.

4. Envision that parents and teenagers will feel great love and appreciation toward their church leaders for inspiring them and teaching them how to rebuild heart connections.

5. Envision that high school seniors will feel gratitude for all those adults who discipled them but will sense special gratitude for their parents who served as their most important disciplers.

6. Envision that parents will feel great love and appreciation for the church leaders who inspired and trained those parents to become the primary disciplers of their own teenagers.

7. Envision that parents and teenagers with reconnected hearts will experience intimate and vibrant worship as families.

8. Envision that parents and teenagers with reconnected hearts will experience joyful recreation and fellowship designed by church leaders for families.

9. Envision that families with reconnected hearts will intentionally bring under their roof and influence teenagers who have not met Christ.

10. Envision that parents will create an anticipation in a child that he or she will go to the front lines of missions for a substantial time soon after high school and that parents will begin saving at the birth of that child to fund that adventure.

11. Envision that families will perform acts of ministry and service together, both locally and internationally.

12. Envision that students from spiritually alive homes will, in God's sovereign timing, lead the church into an awakening to Christ for all He is.

13. Envision that parents will champion their teenagers following God's clear call, even if that call should entail sacrifice, risk, or even martyrdom.

The Congregation

Your congregation has a personality. That personality is warm and welcoming to students, cool and distrusting toward them, or somewhere in between. When students visit your church, they probably can detect the general attitude of adults toward them in about fifteen minutes.

Over time you can use what you say in the pulpit or church publications to create a more positive attitude toward students. You can tell brief stories of what Christ is doing in the hearts of students. You can express your own delight in this age group. You can repeat positive things students have said about their church. You can report things students have done to extend the ministry of the church.

You also can lead students to perform ministries that bless the congregation. Serving tables at a senior adult banquet, providing free child care during the Christmas shopping season, and painting murals in the children's area are worthy ministries that also change perceptions of teenagers.

The way the congregation feels about you also will help determine how they feel about students. The senior adult who reports, "That student minister walks by me every Sunday without speaking" will have a different attitude toward the youth group than the one who says, "I couldn't believe the student minister came by our noon luncheon and even played a round of dominoes."

Consider placing a funeral spray of flowers at the front of the auditorium during Sunday worship. Explain to the congregation that the church is observing the passing away of a youth group that once was an appendage to the church. Celebrate the fact that students and adults soon will become a more united church family, enjoying all that the generations have to offer each other.

Volunteers

The new paradigm in student ministry will require connecting students with many more adults than ever before. Does that seem almost impossible to you? Are you finding it so difficult to enlist adults today that you can't imagine finding many more for the future?

This cannot be all on your shoulders. This is one of the reasons all key church leaders must support moving to a new paradigm of student ministry. Many leaders must share with you the responsibility of calling out adults.

The pastor is primary. As he increasingly embraces the supremacy of Christ, he will be in the best position to invite adults to join him on that journey. Small-group leaders for adults also have potential to issue the call.

Here is the key: Only adults who are falling more and more in love with Jesus and increasingly awed by His majesty will respond in significant numbers to a new call on their lives. Need proof? Your church today is probably telling adults they *should* be doing many things, but mostly it isn't working.

If you, the pastor, and other leaders simply try to convince spiritually plateaued adults that it is their *obligation* to work even harder by helping with students, you will be disappointed by the response. Only being "reconverted" back to all Christ is today can provide the joy and zeal that leads adults enthusiastically to become part of new kingdom activity.

As new groups of adults step forward to build heart connections with students, they will become partners with you in ministry. Most never will become trip sponsors, pizza servers, or van drivers. Some will be grandparents. But they must become valuable to you and among the relationships you enjoy and invest in over the years.

Teach your volunteers everything you know about student ministry. Watching them prosper in ministry will bless you beyond knowing more than they know.

Build heart connections with your volunteers. Your ability to impact them hinges as much on relationships as it does with students.

More than anything, awaken your volunteers to more of who Christ is today. Share with them new discoveries you are making about

Him. Invite them into new ways of worshipping and adoring Him with you. Give them books to read. Pray with them into the night. Go on retreats just for them. Take your volunteers on a journey into the supremacy of Christ and then watch for your students to begin coming alive to Him.

Other Matters

Architecture for Student Ministry

Churches that embrace a new paradigm in student ministry and also desire to build space that will include students will begin to ask new questions:

- How will the design of this building reflect our student ministry purpose and philosophy?

- How will it assist in the connecting of hearts between students and their parents?

- How will it strengthen relationships between students and their disciplers?

- How will it build bonds between students and the congregation?

- How will it support students as they live in biblical community with their peers?

Networking

Under the old paradigm of student ministry, leaders often worked in isolation from other leaders in the community. Even worse, some leaders thought they were in competition with the others. (Only those with true kingdom hearts can celebrate when Christ chooses to prosper and multiply the student ministry down the street.)

Under the new paradigm, student ministers link arms with the other leaders in the community who share their calling and passion for the exaltation of Christ. They create or support a local student ministry network because:

- They believe leaders who together implement a broad ministry strategy will win and disciple far more students than they could by working in isolation.

- They believe a local network provides the strongest and most long-lasting support for ministries on all the secondary school campuses.

- They believe all leaders together have better insights into Scripture, students, culture, and ministry than any one could have alone.

- They need the support of soul mates in ministry when discouragement and crisis come.

The National Network of Youth Ministries links youth workers for encouragement, spiritual growth, and sharing resources in order to expose every teenager to the gospel of Jesus Christ, establish those who respond in a local church, and disciple them to help reach the world. This organization can be valuable to you as you create or strengthen a local network of student ministry leaders. To connect with the Network, go to www.youthworkers.net.

A Rock in Your Shoe

A student minister called a student ministry professor to say, "I need help finding a new church to serve. I must be the most unlucky student minister on earth. Can you believe I have been fired by the third church in a row? And on top of that, all three firings took place in the first year or two. What are the odds that I would be called to three dysfunctional churches one after another?"

It is slightly possible the caller had gone to three unhealthy churches in a row—and that they all fired him without cause. It is far more likely that he is not aware of things he does that almost always lead to a breakdown in relationships.

Even some student ministers who do not get fired go through years of frustration. Honestly, some never have a clue what the real issues are. One might say, "I have some of the most spiritually uncommitted volunteers on earth." But it could well be the student minister's blind spots and personal issues that have caused volunteers to pull back. Another student minister may say, "I would never have come here if I had known the parents were backstabbers." In reality the parents might be reacting to repeated breaches of trust with the student minister that the student minister may not even see.

You easily can see blind spots in others. You may not be aware that you have them too. Others likely see them even if you do not.

If you are aware that you do or say things that create problems at home or work, then you must choose what to do next. That issue, probably from your childhood, is similar to a little rock in your shoe. Most people choose just to keep walking with the rock. But as years pass the pain becomes worse and worse. Finally, when their sock becomes wet with blood, they have no choice but to take the rock out.

But you can make a different choice. Even though it is some trouble, you can sit on the curb now and shake the rock out—long before the real bleeding begins. Then you get to enjoy walking the rest of your life. What for you would be the first concrete step to take toward shaking out the rock? Who is the first trustworthy person you should tell that you are ready to move toward healing?

In general, remain vitally interested in your own personality and makeup all your life. Celebrate the good that you have brought from your childhood, but stay interested in discovering the not-so-good that may be tripping you up. Read on the subject. Ask trusted friends for feedback. Every time you look backward and see unpleasant patterns, resolve to do all you can to get insight and to shake out some more rocks.

In some cases it might be secret sin that is causing pain and life disruption. As you consider whether to indulge your temptations, ask yourself:

1. Am I willing to lose the intimate part of my relationship with Christ?

2. Am I willing to become spiritually irrelevant to those closest to me?

3. Am I willing to see innocent people suffer while Christ deals with my sin?

4. Am I willing to endure public humiliation as Christ deals with my sin?

5. Am I willing to become useless in Christ's kingdom expansion?

You cannot afford what sin costs. Choose to experience grace, create accountability, and ask Christ to give you a breastplate of righteousness.

Am I Going to Like This?

You might be asking, "If I lead my church toward a new paradigm of student ministry, will I enjoy my new role?" There are no guarantees, but here is the probable answer. If you experience a new awakening to the supremacy of Christ and you begin to adore Him in entirely new ways, then you are about to go on the grandest adventure of your life. In a year or two you may be praying prayers similar to these:

Jesus, I am experiencing far greater joy
watching students flock around Your throne
than I did watching them flock around me.

I love seeing joy instead of emptiness in eyes of my students
now that their homes are better.

I love hearing students honor parents for being their most important
spiritual leaders much more than when some gave that honor to me.

I delight in seeing my volunteers increasingly embracing Christ
and becoming more skilled in their leadership roles.

I am blessed by the students they disciple who are
looking more and more like Jesus.

I smile when I see many students and members of the congregation
who now pause for hugs and whispered prayers together.

King Jesus, now I see every indication that most of these students will
continue on kingdom adventures with You all of their lives.

For Your name and glory, nothing could please me more.

Chapter Eleven
Students

Relationships form the foundation for all ministry. Perhaps that is doubly true for student ministry. Guiding teenagers into increasingly deeper relationships with other teenagers should be a priority for any student minister. Teenagers are spiritually transformed through relationships with other believing peers. They are strengthened in lifestyle choices by friends who live in righteousness. Teenagers are more likely to stay on mission with Christ for a lifetime when their closest associates are strong believers. A youth group filled with warmth and love tends to draw in teenagers who have not yet met Christ.

The good news is, virtually every leader knows relationships among the teenagers must be a central focus of student ministry. Consequently, more has been written about this facet of ministry than any other. Therefore, the remainder of this chapter will focus more on relationships between teenagers and adults.

Your Relationships with Students

Relationships form the foundation for ministry. Therefore, relationships are more important than administrative detail. But if administrative detail is neglected, chaos finally will escalate until relationships are damaged. The key is not to decide *whether* to focus on relationships or administration but to know *when* to focus on them.

Wise leaders give attention to administration and preparation when students are not present so that when students are present they get leaders' full attention. Staff and volunteers ought to have their act together before the first students arrive for any gathering. The payoff for arriving early and having administration out of the way is giving undivided attention to students.

Fellowship among staff and volunteers is valuable, but it needs to happen at other times than when students are arriving. Fellowshipping staff and volunteers who segregate from students are just perpetuating the estrangement of teenagers from meaningful adult relationships.

Adults must be careful not to minister most to those who need it least. Staff and volunteers who actively pursue relationships during unstructured time need to follow Jesus' example. In informal gatherings He always seemed to gravitate toward those who needed Him most. "It is not those who are healthy who need a physician, but those who are sick" (Matt. 9:12).

Student ministers and volunteers who do not follow His lead will tend to gravitate toward students who stroke leaders' egos, carry on the wittiest conversations, or are the most attractive. If Jesus were a student ministry volunteer today, He likely would gravitate toward those who are in too much pain to build up adult egos, too slow to be sharp in conversation, or not physically appealing enough to attract adult interest.

Maximizing Conversations

Adults who disciple three students get to enjoy long conversations with those three. Family members who take measures to simplify schedules also get to talk at length. But student ministers must maximize the positive values of shorter conversations.

That does not mean every conversation with every student must be serious or only include religious vocabulary. It does mean every conversation should have value. Because the number of sentences you can exchange with a given student on a given day may be so few, every one of them should build up, encourage, challenge, affirm, inspire, instruct, or do something else that has importance.

Students Relating to Adults

Because this book is targeted to adults, it emphasizes adult initiatives to establish heart connections with students. But in reality both generations need to take steps toward the other.

The creation of a youth culture that would exist separately from the mainstream culture was dysfunctional. The church mimicking that dysfunctional state of affairs by creating segregated youth groups was a mistake. Even so, teenagers today were born into this system and likely cannot even think of an alternative reality.

Parents and leaders they know and trust will need to help them see a reality that is preferable to the matrix that shapes their world. They will need to say things similar to, "Imagine getting connected to an adult in love with Jesus who has time to listen to some of your deepest questions about your faith." "Think about coming to church knowing a hug and an encouraging word will be waiting for you." "What if you knew a person of deep prayer were bringing your name before heaven every morning while you dressed for school?"

Students who begin to see the value of expanding and deepening adult relationships need one additional challenge. They need the challenge to take some of the initiative in building those relationships. Students are full of relationship potential, and they do not need to be passive, waiting for five key adults to worm their way into their lives.

Leaders placing this challenge before students might say things similar to:

- "If your parent shows a little interest in gathering the family for worship, respond immediately. Your parent may feel insecure about leading out and may even wonder if the family will ridicule the idea. A quick, positive response from you might be just what your parent needs to have the confidence to move forward."

- "When you first meet your prayer mentor this Sunday, show just as much interest in your partner's life as he or she shows in yours. Here are some great questions to ask an older adult. . . ."

- "Your new discipler might express interest in your family and interests. Plan to return the favor. Here are some creative ways you can reach out to your discipler and know him or her as a person. . . ."

As both generations begin to invest in relationships, the age of segregated student groups will come to an end. Arm in arm, students and adults increasingly will wake up to much more of who the Son of the Most High is today and *together* will arise to join Him in changing the world.

Two-Way Spiritual Impact

An awakening to Christ may well begin among adults. Parents and leaders with heart connections with students may spark that same awakening in a young generation. *But not necessarily.* God is sovereign, and He can do what He pleases. He may choose to exalt His Son first among students.

If He does, awakening will spread most rapidly in homes and churches where relationships between the generations already are warm and strong. Those heart connections then become the conduit through which the Spirit carries spiritual life and renewal to the entire congregation.

Churches in the U.S. stood in great need of awakening at the end of the tumultuous 1960s. God fanned into flames the Jesus Movement among students in 1970. He focused all the attention on His Son Jesus. Hippies were so captivated by the love young believers held toward Christ that tens of thousands joined His eternal family.

But the power and wonder of that season never spread through the church at large. High on the list of reasons was the absence of relationships. Because few adults had heart connections with young believers, they gave all their energy to complaining about sandals and jeans on Sunday and Jesus cheers and long hair in the sanctuary. The kindling of awakening, now pushed away from the logs, soon died. Churches that continue to segregate teenagers and the full congregation increase the likelihood the same thing could happen again.

No one knows where the Spirit will ignite the spark next. But if the entire body of Christ is living in relationships, then the flame can spread regardless.

Students Leading Student Ministry

One of the great strengths of contemporary student ministry is the skill and competence of adult leaders. One of the great dangers of contemporary student ministry is that skilled leaders will do it all and thus will leave students as passive participants.

Students are not the church of tomorrow. They are the church today. To be effective leaders tomorrow, they need to lead today. It is a mistake to do for a student what that student is capable of doing. Johnny Derouen, now a professor of student ministry, was student minister at a church selected as "exemplary" in a nationwide study (www.exemplarym.com). He reports his approach to ministry was, "I taught them how to do ministry and let them do ministry. I gave it back to them, and it was their ministry."

Every parent and adult who relates to teenagers should consider this process:

- I do it (briefly) and you observe.
- I do most of it and you do some.
- You do most of it and I do some.
- You do all of it and I coach.
- For the rest of your life, you do it.

This is the pattern Jesus used for three years with His apostles and with the seventy He sent out two by two (Luke 10).

Parents

Chapter 12 makes clear that wise parents will open doors for their teenagers to take spiritual leadership roles in the home. Parents and siblings can benefit spiritually from strengths often present with teenagers. Parents should give students active leadership roles in family worship. Families that follow the family worship plans at www. heartconnex.org will find the teenager in a leadership role every time the family gathers.

The Discipler

Chapter 9 makes clear that one-on-three discipleship does not leave students in a passive role. Leaders have a clear expectation that each student will have a role in the transformation of the other students *and* the adult. In the high school years even the formal leadership of the group shifts more and more to the students. By the time students graduate from high school, they should be fully prepared to disciple future disciple makers on their college campus, military base, or in the workplace.

The Prayer Mentor

Chapter 7 makes clear that a student and a seasoned saint in a prayer partner relationship are to bless each other. Students are just as responsible for investing in the relationship as the adults. Students are just as responsible for praying concertedly for their partners. They are just as responsible for offering care and ministry to their partners. In such relationships older adults are just as likely to be built up in the faith as are the teenagers.

Core Planning Team

Chapter 6 makes clear that students are to be well represented on the core planning team. The core planning team shapes the student ministry plan and calendar for the coming year. This team is composed of core students, parents, and volunteers who are spiritually transformed and sensitive to the Spirit's leading, who have the student ministry purpose statement in their DNA, and who are adept in strategic planning. Planning *with* students is of far greater value than planning *for* students.

Lead Teams

Chapter 6 also makes clear that students are to be well represented on lead teams. Lead teams serve to implement events or projects calendared by the core planning team. Examples include youth camp, a retreat, an all-night prayer gathering, or a family remodeling project at the rescue mission. Lead teams are composed of students, parents, and volunteers. They are a practical way to mobilize many students in crafting their own student ministry.

Spiritual Markers and Developmental Stages

Jesus never has created two snowflakes or two teenagers exactly the same. Pubescent teenagers do not become curvy exactly on the same schedule, and they are not spiritually transformed on the same schedule. At the same time, general patterns of mental and emotional development seem to open the door to elements of spiritual development.

Seventh Graders—Identity

Many seventh graders believe:

- I am of little value since my body does not match the stereotypes of society.

- I am of little value since the timetable for my sexual development is different from others.

- I am of little value since I cannot yet identify my gifts, strengths, and abilities.

- I am just the product of random chance at the time of my conception.

Seventh grade is an important year in establishing identity. Scars that last a lifetime can occur as teenagers come to negative conclusions about their bodies, abilities, and related issues. Humanistic explanations about their worth and value can sound hollow.

But what if seventh graders are surrounded with people who are coming more and more alive to the Lord Jesus Christ? What if they are in churches moving from spiritual lethargy to spiritual vibrancy?

Those seventh graders can have a very different experience. As they peer into the DNA of at least five adults with whom they share life, they can see identities grounded in Christ. Who those adults *are* will simply amplify and confirm what they teach from Scripture about true identity. And beyond those five primary relationships, seventh graders who are valued by a Christ-focused congregation can come to more positive conclusions of their intrinsic worth.

By the end of their seventh-grade year, teenagers should affirm:

- My identity is centered in who I am in King Jesus.

- I was designed in the mind of Christ before the foundation of the world.

- Christ is all-brilliant and all-powerful, and thus all He creates is right and good.

- The way Christ designed me perfectly fits His plans and purposes for me.

- I am royalty because of my relationship with the Monarch, and I will reign with Him some day.

Illustrative Scripture: "I will give thanks to You, for I am fearfully and wonderfully made; wonderful are Your works, and my soul knows it very well" (Ps. 139:14).

Eighth Graders—Purpose

Many eighth graders believe:

- Because I am a product of evolutionary chance, my life has no purpose.

- My highest goal is to find happiness and peace of mind.

- My most important activity is gathering possessions.

- God is not very important in my daily life unless I happen to need Him to make me happy or trouble-free.

Seventh graders secure in a biblical view of their identity are ready to discover their purpose in the eighth grade. Through heart connections with adults who have been "reconverted" back to who Christ really is today, they can find their biblical reason for being on earth. They can discover they are here to arise to join Christ in bringing His kingdom on earth for His fame and glory. The decision in eighth grade to live (or even die) for the glory of Christ shapes immediate decisions they must make concerning family, friends, the church, and the world.

By the end of their eigth-grade year, teenagers should affirm:

- Jesus Christ has a unique plan for my life.

- My highest purpose is to live or die for the glory of Christ.

- My most important activity is allowing Christ to live His life through me as He brings His kingdom on earth.

- My greatest desire is to see all peoples worship and give praise to God.

- My greatest joy comes when I am in the center of Christ's purposes.

Illustrative Scripture: "Praise the LORD, all nations; laud Him, all peoples!" (Ps. 117:1).

Ninth Graders—Core Beliefs

Many ninth graders believe:

- All religious writings have about the same value.

- I leave the articulating of beliefs to my parents and church leaders.

- I feel too close-minded if I try to defend my faith.

The increasing ability to think abstractly gives ninth graders the ability to assimilate beliefs they have heard from others. This also is a period when the brain begins to slough off and absorb potential neural connections that never have been used. The issue becomes "use it or lose it." It is essential for ninth graders to internalize, assimilate, and articulate the basics of faith while their brains are poised for the process.

In some churches Bible teaching and faith formation are dead and lifeless. But churches experiencing a rebirth of devotion to Christ Himself are at very different places. Rediscovering the majesty of Jesus leads to a rediscovery of the majesty, power, and life of His written Word. A fascination with the Author leads to a fascination with His Book.

Spiritually alive parents and leaders can assist ninth graders in moving from Bible facts to understanding, from hearing what others believe to embracing truth themselves, and moving from difficulty articulating truth to clearly expressing their most basic beliefs.

By the end of ninth grade, teenagers should affirm:

- God's Word is truth and thus forms the basis for all I believe and do.

- My worldview is centered in Scripture.

- All I know of Christ and my relationship with Him is consistent with His written Word.

- I can put into words my most basic beliefs.

- I can give a reasoned defense of my faith.

Illustrative Scripture: "Sanctify Christ as Lord in your hearts, always being ready to make a defense to everyone who asks you to give an account for the hope that is in you, yet with gentleness and reverence" (1 Pet. 3:15).

Tenth Graders—Freedom

Many tenth graders believe:

- I am most free when I follow my own desires without regard for Christ or others.

- This is a time in life to pursue freedom and reject responsibility.

- Disobeying those in authority leads to freedom.

- Disobeying those in authority proves I am growing up.

Balancing freedom and responsibility is a central issue for tenth graders. Automobile driving brings new freedom away from parents and new moral pressures. The cost of driving can motivate some tenth graders to allow part-time employment to rule over all other life issues. Control is beginning to shift from direct parental supervision to an internal moral compass. Peers can give tenth graders conflicting or even erroneous guidance.

Parents and leaders in warm relationships with students can show them that license leads to slavery while thinking and acting like Christ leads to true freedom. But even then leaders sometimes become frustrated and say, "I teach these teenagers the truth every week, and then they go out and live just the opposite."

As students begin to adore Christ more and more deeply, their decision-making processes begin to change. Sixteen years of Bible teaching gives them the knowledge they need to live righteously. Growing awe, respect, and intimacy with the Son of God gives them the *will* to live out what they know to be true.

By the end of tenth grade, teenagers should affirm:

- I am most free when I live in conformity with the supremely majestic Jesus Christ.

- Balancing freedom and responsibility is central to my decision-making.

- I love and value those in authority for they enable me better to achieve my kingdom purposes.

Illustrative Scripture: "I run in the path of your commands, for you have set my heart free. . . . I will walk about in freedom, for I have sought out your precepts" (Ps. 119:32, 45 NIV).

Eleventh Graders—the Future

Many eleventh graders believe:

- Every decision I make about the future should assist me in finding happiness and peace of mind.

- He who dies with the most toys wins, and I plan to win.

Concerns about careers and college once associated with the senior year now have been pushed down to eleventh grade. Society increasingly pressures juniors to declare their specific plans for undergraduate education, vocational training, or military service. This presses Christian juniors to give early thought to choosing a vocation and life path under God's leadership.

Christian educators are familiar with the progression of think, feel, and do. With regards to Christ, this becomes:

- **Think**: *Awake* to the full extent of who Christ is today.

- **Feel**: *Adore* Him in all His majesty (with this adoration based on what was discovered in an awakening to Him).

- **Do**: *Arise* to join Him in His kingdom purposes (flowing out of the power of adoration to influence the will). (Remember all doing flows from being.)

Sixteen-year-olds in homes and churches becoming alive to Christ likely have had many opportunities to *awake* and *adore*. Their junior year is the time for them to consider how *arising* to join Christ in what He is doing in the world can influence their plans for education and vocation.

By the end of eleventh grade, teenagers should affirm:

- As Christ lives out His life through me, I will achieve the reason for my existence.

- He is willing and able to reveal to me the next step I am to take in following His unique plan for my life.

- Achieving power, prestige, or possessions is of no importance compared to the joy of knowing Christ and joining Him in His kingdom purposes.

- I know His plans for me will include telling all peoples about Him.

Illustrative Scripture: "'For I know the plans that I have for you,' declares the LORD, 'plans for welfare and not for calamity to give you a future and a hope'" (Jer. 29:11).

Twelfth Graders—Absolute Truth

Many twelfth graders believe:

- All truth is relative.
- It does not matter what you believe as long as you are sincere.
- All "holy" books have equal authority.
- All religions point people to the same God, and all their sincere adherents will spend eternity with Him.

After high school graduation, most students are challenged strongly to abandon the faith they grew up with. At the very least, they are challenged to acknowledge their faith is just one of many equally true and useful religious perspectives. They also are challenged to doubt whether absolute truth or moral authority exists in the universe. The senior year is the last opportunity to prepare them for these powerful assaults on their faith in college and beyond.

Seniors do not finalize a faith that will last by filling in blanks in a handout or passively listening to speakers. They hammer out their faith as they question and probe and analyze. These higher levels of learning require seniors to be in active conversation with adults of deep faith. If churches place more than three seniors in a learning session with one adult, then some seniors must become passive simply by virtue of time. Learners who are the most passive are most at risk of not experiencing lasting transformation. Perhaps more than for any other year, seniors need to be in close relationship with two parents and three other adults who are alive in Christ.

By the end of twelfth grade, teenagers should affirm:

- God's Word is absolute truth and thus forms the sole basis for my worldview.

- The plan of redemption in the Bible is the only one available to humankind.

- Sincere, faithful, and moral adherents to any nonbiblical religion will spend eternity in hell.

- When the Bible contradicts other truth claims, those claims are false.

- The Bible is the only repository of God's written truth to humankind.

Illustrative Scripture: "Sanctify them in the truth; Your word is truth" (John 17:17).

To see a Christ-focused curriculum built on these six developmental themes, go to www.oneonthree.com.

Closing

Churches experiencing an awakening to much more of who Christ is today—gathering worshippers adoring His Majesty, filled with conversations about arising to join the King in new kingdom adventures, composed of families taking the lead in spiritual impact—could experience:

- Students becoming more faithful in attendance and taking more leadership every year.

- Students becoming more bold and passionate for the kingdom every year.

- Students giving more evidence every year that theirs is a lifetime faith.

Chapter Twelve
Parents

Parents who are decent people but do not know Christ generally want their children to become adults who:

- Are happy.
- Work hard and are financially independent.
- Live as good citizens and obey the law.
- Relate to spouses, children, and extended family in a warm, loving way.

What about the parents in your church or ministry? Are their goals for child-rearing much different from the goals held by people without Christ?

Spiritually shallow parents would just add that they want their children to become adults who:

- Consider themselves Christians.
- Attend church.
- Live morally.

But what if there were an awakening among your parents? What if parents started longing to see something in young adults leaving their home that goes beyond just occupying a church pew? What if parents increasingly had this goal for their teenagers?

Students who, for the glory of the Father and in the power of the Spirit, spend a lifetime
embracing the full supremacy of the Son,
responding to His majesty in all of life,
inviting Christ to live His life through them,
and joining Him in making disciples among all peoples.

Teenagers with Spiritually Shallow Parents

- Most children and teenagers reared by Christ-adoring parents become Christ-adoring young adults.

- Most children and teenagers reared by parents without Christ become young adults without Christ.

- Many children and teenagers reared in spiritually shallow homes become spiritually shallow young adults.

But not all do.

A fair percentage of those reared in spiritually shallow homes walk away from the faith altogether as young adults. Watching parents who attend church but who do not fully embrace Christ and His kingdom confuses them and even turns them against the faith.

Parents awaking to the supremacy of Jesus, *parents* more deeply adoring Him on His throne, and *parents* daily arising to join Him in His kingdom activity offer the brightest hope for teenagers moving in those same directions.

The Spiritual Leadership of Parents

Parents' spiritual leadership in the home always has been God's ideal. Just listen: "These words, which I am commanding you today, shall be on your heart. You shall teach them diligently to your sons and shall talk of them when you sit in your house and when you walk by the way and when you lie down and when you rise up" (Deut. 6:6–7).

He commanded our fathers,
That they should make them known to their children;
That the generation to come might know them,
The children who would be born,
That they may arise and declare them to their children,
That they may set their hope in God,
And not forget the works of God,
But keep His commandments (Ps. 78:5–7 NKJV).

God's *primary* plan for getting truth into the lives of children and teenagers is at the feet of their parents. Brian Haynes, the visionary behind the milestones approach to family ministry, often says,

> "Connecting faith and home is more than a model or strategy.
> It is a movement of God in our day."

Taking teenagers to church is important, but it cannot take the place of parents as disciplers. The following "logic" is flawed:

Question: Are you helping your high school student with advanced math homework?

Parent: No, but through my taxes I am paying someone to do that for me. I'm fine with that.

Question: Are you teaching your high schooler the things of God?

Parent: No, but through my tithe I am paying someone to do that for me. I'm fine with that."

Parents who want to see their children delight in Christ all their lives should:

- Have a deep appreciation for vocational ministers and church leaders who impact their children.

- Work aggressively to deepen relationships between their children and those church leaders.

- Build family schedules around the ministries and services of the church.

- Become firm supporters of all the church is doing to impact their children spiritually.

But at the same time parents should never abdicate to the church the final responsibility for the spiritual instruction of their children. Parents accept the call to lead their children spiritually because:

- They honor Christ in their homes because He is the sovereign Lord of the universe.

- They joyfully accept His authority because they revere Him, love Him, and have a heart of gratitude toward Him.

- They embrace His principles of parenting and family life because He is God and because they know His precepts offer the only hope for a spiritually and emotionally healthy family.

Actually, parents *will* lead children spiritually, one direction or another. The faith of the children almost always will mirror that of parents. Parents have to decide if that is good news or bad news for their families. The research is clear:

National Study of Youth and Religion: "The evidence clearly shows that the single most important social influence on the religious and spiritual lives of adolescents is their parents. Grandparents and other relatives, mentors, and youth workers can be very influential as well. But normally parents are most important in forming their children's religious and spiritual lives."[1]

Researchers Merton P. Strommen and Richard A. Hardel: "Though a child may be strongly influenced by his or her friends, the power of this peer group emerges as dominant only when the relationship of love with parents is vastly diminished. Caring parents are the primary influence in shaping the moral values of their children."[2]

Informal and Formal Spiritual Instruction

Read again Deuteronomy 6:6–7: "These words, which I am commanding you today, shall be on your heart. You shall teach them diligently to your sons and shall talk of them *when you sit in your house* and *when you walk by the way* and *when you lie down and when you rise up*" (emphasis added).

Parents provide spiritual instruction in their home both formally and informally. "When you sit in your house" suggests formal instruction, something that is planned and prepared for. "When you walk by the way" sounds less formal and even spontaneous. Both are vital. When you "lie down" and "rise up" suggests making a child's waking up and going to sleep spiritually meaningful.

Informal spiritual impact takes place as parents model truth and values in front of their children. It includes talks in the van on the way to soccer and searching Scripture together when a child has a crisis. It even includes the sparkle in parents' eyes as they tell children new discoveries they are making about who Christ really is today.

Regularly children should hear parents say:

- Come sit down over here. I want to share with you something new Christ is doing in my life right now.

- I have been looking forward to breakfast this morning because I want to tell you what the Holy Spirit showed me in Scripture during my quiet time early this morning.

- The truth of that sermon hit me hard this morning. Son, you need to know what I committed to God at the close of the service.

Informal spiritual instruction in the home is vital but never can take the place of formal times the family gathers to talk of the things of God. Parents might need a guide to know how best to plan family Bible study and worship. They also may profit from printed guidance in knowing how to make timeless truths come alive for a new generation.

Parents need a printed plan that:

- Has an overarching approach to present the full counsel of Scripture over a period of time.

- Has creative approaches that make Bible teaching relevant and interesting to the ages of children.

- Has creative ways to make family worship warm, intimate, and relational.

- Has a variety of ways for the family to pray together.

One such plan is located at www.heartconnex.org.

Teenagers learn and absorb priorities more from what parents do than from what they say. If parents allow other activities to squeeze out family worship, they will have taught a permanent lesson about what *really* is most important in the home. When teenagers parent their own children some day, they likely will follow the same pattern.

Parents bring additional spiritual impact to teenagers when they make waking up or bedtime spiritually meaningful. Deuteronomy 6:7 calls parents to bring blessing to children "when you lie down and when you rise up." Family worship at the beginning or end of the day meets this need. If family worship is another time, parents can make a habit of saying or doing something as each child wakes up or is about to go to sleep that turns hearts toward Christ.

Scripture is clear. God calls dads who know Jesus to serve as the spiritual leaders of their homes. He also has a plan for all families. Scripture makes clear that God has a special heart for single mothers. God gives them the privilege of serving as the spiritual leader to their children or even grandchildren. He promises to equip them fully for this task.

Mothers whose husbands have not yet met Christ long for them to meet Jesus and to move into the role of spiritual leader. Until then Christ invites mothers courageously to stand in the gap as spiritual leader. He will fully equip them with all they need for the task.

Praying as Families

Family prayer must be a part of formal spiritual instruction. Prayer during family worship and devotionals will seem more natural if parents pray with children every night. Praying with toddlers at bedtime seems comfortable to most Christian parents, but seventeen-year-olds need it just as much (and perhaps more).

Prayer during family times must have variety. Too much predictable sameness makes prayer seem like a ritual. Families need to think of new ways to pray, new places to pray, and new words in prayer.

Family prayers should include prayer for one another. Parents may find it meaningful to stand behind children with hands on their shoulders or head while praying over them. Children can do just the same over parents and siblings.

As with any prayer group, families should be faithful in recording their prayers of intercession so later they can record the ways God chose to answer. Such journaling teaches children a life-altering lesson about the power of prayer.

Spiritual instruction and impact in the home lack power without prayer. Some prayer concerns parents can only express in private. But the complement to private prayer is prayer children get to hear.

- Children and teenagers must hear parents bringing them before Christ.

- They need to hear the depth of parents' love revealed in those prayers.

- They need to hear how keenly parents want to see impact radiating out from their lives.

- They need to hear parents release them to God's call and purposes.

Hearing such prayers may be one of the most important experiences children can have.

Discipline

In some homes adult self-fulfillment and stress-avoidance take precedence over the demanding work of disciplining children. Children who stay on mission with Christ for a lifetime seldom come from homes with weak discipline.

Modeling God's justice means parents are in authority over their children (Prov. 6:20; 19:18). Parents make decisions about structure, limits, and behavior; and they enforce those decisions. Parents never stop parenting, even when emotionally tired.

When older children and teens pull against decisions and structure, parents hold the rope. They dole out more rope as kids show growing maturity and responsibility, but they never turn loose completely.

Here is a paradox:

- The parent who chooses to be a buddy instead of a parent likely will not end up with a buddy but with an estranged teenager or young adult. On top of that, parents who try to be buddies seldom rear children focused on Christ's kingdom.

- The parent who chooses to be a parent instead of a buddy likely will end up with a warm, lifetime friendship with that child. On top of that, godly parents who parent are most likely to rear children who join Christ on kingdom adventures.

Using Consequences to Discipline

Many parents respond to disobedience with emotional outbursts. Usually those are weak responses with limited impact.

Yelling
- Is a choice. No child can make a parent yell.
- Is a sign of an emotional weakness in the parent.
- Usually mimics the yelling a parent's parent practiced.

- Frightens children when supposedly strong parents lose emotional control.

- Damages a child's self-esteem.

- Pushes children away.

- Leads to emotional injuries that can last for years.

- Makes restoring closeness later much more difficult.

- Seldom leads a child or teenager to a permanent change of heart.

- Leads children to become cold, distant teenagers.

Parents who want kingdom kids to emerge from their homes will stop using emotional outbursts as their typical response to bad behavior. "Fathers, do not provoke your children to anger, but bring them up in the discipline and instruction of the Lord" (Eph. 6:4). Connecting bad behavior with negative consequences (discipline) is far more effective than sharp words in changing the behavior.

Parents also need to show children every time their good, biblical choices lead to positive, natural consequences. And parents need to create positive rewards in response to other good choices. Highlighting positives is just as important as giving attention to negative consequences.

Parents parent best when parenting mirrors the way the Father parents them. He parents adults with a perfect balance of His justice and grace.

Modeling God's justice means parents are in authority over children. Parents make decisions about structure, limits, and behavior; and they enforce those decisions.

Modeling God's grace means parents love teenagers without conditions. They communicate that teenagers do not need to do anything, change anything, or accomplish anything to earn parents' love and acceptance. Parents show genuine interest and empathy in their lives, and they establish their well-being as one of parents' highest priorities.

When parents (or student ministers) are being as sinful as they ever get, does God withdraw His love from them? Parents may break the heart of God, and they certainly will experience His discipline, but His love is unfailing (Ps. 51:1). Parents' love for children should be the same. Parents deal with problem behavior with discipline, but their love is unconditional.

Parenting offers no guarantees. But if parents parent with God's balance of justice and grace and their life exudes the supremacy of Christ, then their teenagers likely will love and worship the Father for a lifetime, increasingly will embrace the full supremacy of the Son, and will live to make disciples for Him among all peoples.

Give Teenagers a Heart for the World

A teenager's closest circle of friends should be growing Christians. The older children grow, the more powerful the influence of that inner circle will become. This same principle applies to those a teenager dates or courts. They must be maturing Christians, or harm usually will follow.

Rearing teenagers with hearts for the world begins with their first having hearts for people near at hand without Christ. Christian teenagers in firm relationships with an inner circle of other strong Christians can safely reach out to peers who do not know Christ. In essence, those Christian friends become a rescue squad, holding onto and supporting one another as they reach across the quicksand to friends who need Jesus.

Some church parents fearful of the world try to isolate their children from people without Christ. Those same parents probably hope their children will grow up to be strong adults who then will try to win the world to Jesus. Unfortunately, parents have no magic switch to throw to change an older teen's mind-set from "avoid people without Christ at all costs" to "redeem all persons to Christ."

Children who can't remember a time when family members weren't focused on friends and acquaintances without Christ probably will grow into young adults with a heart for the world. A heart for their

"Jerusalem" may lead easily to a concern for the "uttermost part of the earth" (Acts 1:8 KJV).

Family Missions

Parents who perform acts of missions and service with their children make a lifetime impact on those children. In fact, research suggests missions and service are better predictors of their faith maturity as adults than participation in Bible study or worship services.[3]

This research does not suggest church Bible study and worship are unimportant. They are foundational for any believing family. The research does suggest, though, that the most kingdom-focused young adults tend to have experienced missions and service with their families while young. Parents who never do such activities with their children or teenagers are missing one of their most powerful opportunities for impact.

God is calling families to missions locally, nationally, and globally. Parents may need to partner with church leaders to become knowledgeable about opportunities for their family in each arena. Serving Thanksgiving dinner at the rescue mission or traveling to a Third-World country can be powerful steps moving an entire family toward the supremacy of Christ.

Family Finances

Family mission trips nationally and globally require money. God may be calling families to choose to live more frugally than necessary in order to release unusual funds for the glory of Christ. Some years an international mission trip as a family may take priority over the newest high-definition, big-screen television.

Wise parents involve children and teenagers in making decisions about finances. A family meeting might include questions such as:

- Since our family has more than enough food, how much do each of you suggest we commit to ministry with starving people each month?

- Who would be willing to do a Web search of organizations that assist starving people in the name of Jesus Christ?

- What can each of you suggest we cut back on so we will have enough money to commit to feeding programs and to traveling to minister directly with starving people ourselves?

Family Prayer for the World

Children growing up praying about global kingdom issues are likely to become kingdom-focused young adults. Wise parents include prayer for the nations and for kingdom concerns when the family gathers for study and worship. Wise student ministers provide printed and Internet sources for fresh prayer needs locally and globally.

Television and Other Media

Church parents sometimes say:

- I know we should be praying and studying as Christian families, but honestly we can't find even 15 minutes for such gatherings.

- I know doing a service project as a family would be memorable, but where in our feverish schedule would that ever fit?

- I know I need to go to my kids' bedrooms more often for long talks, but all I have time for is just the basics to keep our home operating.

Somehow the math does not add up. The average adult watches television two hours and thirty-eight minutes per day. Online activities are on top of that. Perhaps parents have more discretionary time than they realize. If parents watched one hour of television an evening, suddenly ninety-eight minutes would be available for family worship, supervising homework projects, crafting wise discipline, and listening to the hearts of children.

A family will not reach its potential as a Christ-focused family without managing television and other media.

The Church and the Family

The home is the primary location for the spiritual development of a teenager. Family teaching and modeling are the primary tools for that development. Even though the church is second to the home in importance, it still is indispensible. The King has decreed believers are to assemble (Heb. 10:25). Families who honor and obey Him will do just that.

The Sabbath

Parents and teenagers who embrace the supremacy of Christ take seriously the fourth of the Ten Commandments: "Remember the sabbath day, to keep it holy" (Exod. 20:8). They are just as focused on obeying that commandment as they are those forbidding adultery and murder.

> If parents allow a teenager to skip worship on Sunday morning
> to participate in some activity or competition,
> they have communicated their true priorities to the teenager.

The same is true if parents allow a teenager to take a job that requires Sunday work or they allow him to sleep in after a hard week. Those actions and decisions will make a more lasting impression than what parents try to teach about priorities.

If Christian parents would take a clear stand against allowing their children to participate in activities on Sunday morning, most leagues and other competitions would have no choice but to move to other days and times. At the very least parents and teenagers need to communicate to leaders at the beginning that they will be faithful to every team obligation except Sunday participation.

Relationships

Whether church leaders are people of influence with a teenager depends in large measure on relationships. Relationships depend on consistency. If a teenager is inconsistent in church and youth group involvement, relationships likely will be weak and influence diminished.

A teenager beginning to protest going to church may not be rebellious. He may be revealing that relationships are becoming so weak they do not draw him there. Teenagers live so much in the present that it does not take many scattered absences from church for them to begin to feel distant from leaders and even peers. A teenager's complaints about attending Sundays may be the logical consequence of family decisions to miss now and then.

Parents who make church life a family priority are much more likely to see their children in heart connections with leaders of influence there. They also are likely to see those children equally committed to a local church during college days.

Parents' Partnership with Church Leaders

Many church parents experience shock and awe when they discover they are to be the *primary* spiritual leaders to their children. Most assumed that duty lay with church ministers and leaders. It doesn't.

Parents ready to assume this amazing responsibility need all the help and support they can get. Though church ministers and leaders are not the primary spiritual leaders of teenagers, they can be powerful partners with parents as they fulfill this role.

Deepening Your Awakening to Christ

The most important sentence in this chapter might be this one:

Parents awaking to the supremacy of Jesus, parents more deeply adoring Him on His throne, and parents daily arising to join Him in His kingdom activity offer the brightest hope for teenagers moving in those same directions the rest of their lives.

Student ministers and other leaders who are walking with parents toward that awakening are valuable. Their teaching and preaching should find parents fully engaged as they listen for any new insight that might propel them on the journey. Their opening up to parents new passages of Scripture that reveal more of who Christ is becomes a delight. Their suggesting books and online resources valuable to parents' quest becomes a gift.

True adoration of Christ enthroned will soon cause awakened parents to shout, "Send me!" As that happens, parents can link arms with church leaders who assist believers in finding their own ministries. Parents actively can search out ways to arise to join Jesus in His kingdom activity, locally and globally. Parents who mostly have been pew sitters can bid farewell to that chapter of life as they move out to join Christ on the greatest adventures of their lives.

Think about this:

Perhaps the most powerful thing church leaders can do to give teenagers a sustainable faith is to stimulate *parents'* spiritual pilgrimage.

Now that is a new paradigm.

Training in Parenting

Parents of infants and parents of college students need specific training in parenting. As children grow, parents find themselves parenting every age of child for the first time. Without specific training, most parents tend to reproduce the (sometimes) failed parenting approaches their own parents may have used. Parents need to partner with church leaders in designing training events that provide instruction in both parenting and spiritual leadership.

You and the parents can plan gatherings to address such issues as:

- Discipline
- Sexual purity
- Communication
- The influence of friends
- Understanding youth culture
- The dark side of the online world
- Students and vocational direction
- Finding balance in family schedules
- Keeping marriages vibrant while parenting

- Recognizing and responding to crisis issues
- Transitions to middle school, high school, and college
- Honoring rites of passage (thirteenth birthday, drivers' license, etc.)
- Creative ways to worship as a family
- Sharing truth in the flow of family life
- Using journaling to bless your teenager
- Teaching your teenager new ways to pray
- Global missions opportunities for families
- Local service and ministry opportunities for families
- Ideas for making family Bible study transformational

A megachurch might invest a thousand dollars in a gathering for hundreds of parents on one of these topics. A small church might only invest encouragement as three parents gather to sharpen one another with their insights, to support one another by linking arms, and to strengthen one another through prayer. Both gatherings can be valuable.

Milestones

Many churches recognize their students who are graduating from high school. Church leaders often are surprised to see parents they seldom see attend that service. Milestones in a child's life (such as baby dedication or a child's baptism) often create unusual interest and motivation for parents. Wise churches capitalize on those milestones to draw parents and families into transformational experiences. For information on this approach to impacting families, see www.legacymilestones.com.

Parent and Student Programming

The new student ministry paradigm places high value on intergenerational programming. Possibilities include:

- Family service projects

- Family mission trips (state, national, and global)
- Family social recreation
- Family athletics
- Family camp
- Family retreats
- Family prayer gatherings
- Family worship
- Family cell groups
- Family Bible studies
- Family ceremonies to celebrate rites of passage
- Family ceremonies to celebrate True Love Waits promises of purity
- Graduation dinners
- Parent appreciation banquets

How should parents and leaders feel when moving in these directions and some teenagers ask, "What could be worse than a retreat with parents?" Leaders should remember that a dysfunctional culture has had sixty years to say to teenagers it is best to live surrounded by friends and distant from adults. Leaders can't expect teenagers to change their thinking over night.

The quickest way to change their thinking is to create a reputation for quality whenever families gather. Soon teenagers will be saying: "I thought the retreat was going to be so lame. But it was a blast. The games were the best we ever had, and I loved the late-night prayers. To be honest, I never really knew my dad's prayers were so deep."

Small Group/Sunday School Class/Cell Group for Parents

Parents can partner with leaders to start a new class or group targeted specifically to parents of teenagers. This would not be a parenting class specifically but would follow the same curriculum as the other classes and groups.

A class or group composed of parents of teenagers can become a support for those parents. They can become a "cord of three strands" that is not easily broken (Eccl. 4:12). They also can target some of their prayers toward their own teenagers, the student ministry of the church, and this generation of teenagers.

The group also can approach any passage of Scripture in the curriculum from the unique perspective of parents. Three questions always can be part of the conversation:

- Is there a truth here I can live out in new ways before my children?

- Is there a truth here that can help shape how I am parenting?

- What are ways I can build this truth into the hearts of my children?

Parental Input in the Design of Student Ministry

Parents in the church have hopes and dreams for their teenagers. Most want their children to adore and live for Christ, and they want the same for their generation. Many of their hopes and dreams can be expressed through the student ministry of the church. Parents who are becoming more alive to Christ need ways to help shape the direction of that ministry. Student ministers who are discovering how central parents are to the spiritual lives of teenagers will welcome that involvement. Here are several ways such involvement can happen.

Purpose Statement Design Team—Several parents can become part of a team that will craft a student ministry purpose statement. This statement will define the DNA of the student ministry and will shape all planning for the future. (See chapter 6.)

Core Planning Team—Several parents can become part of a team that will choose programs, events, and ministries for the coming year. They will select programming that flows out of the purpose statement and the ministry priorities selected for that year. (See chapter 6.)

Parent Advisory Team—Several parents can become part of a team that meets several times a year with the student minister. They serve to provide parental wisdom and perspective to those who shape student ministry. They are not a decision-making body, but their recommendations and cautions carry much weight with leaders. For an expanded look at such teams, see Steve Wright's model on page 175 of his book *rethink* (InQuest Publishing).

Parents on Lead Teams—Lead teams are an ongoing way for parents to help shape major events and ministries during the year. They also represent the most time-efficient way for parents to provide logistical support for student ministry. In some churches parents who want to support and help are not sure how to step forward and get involved. In churches with lead teams, parents have a clear way to use their gifts and interests to bless teenagers, families, and volunteers. (See chapter 6.)

Town Hall Meetings—Many parents can participate in large meetings that bring together most active teenagers, parents, and volunteers. The student minister can provide town hall meetings as an efficient way to capture the thinking of a broader audience related to future directions.

Heart Connections between Parents and Teenagers

Relationships are central to making a spiritual impact on children. Children and teenagers tend to embrace parents' faith if parents have heart connections with them. Josh McDowell has it right when he says, "Parents might be spouting biblical truths at their kids, but where's the relationship? Truth without relationship leads to rejection. We are losing our kids not because they don't hear the truth, but because the people speaking the truth haven't spent the time to build relationships with them."[4]

A heart connection is the "pipeline" that connects the hearts of parent and child. Through that pipeline spiritual impact flows from one generation to the next. Parents who keep that heart connection warm and strong usually see visible evidence that their faith and values are passing to their children. "And he will turn (connect) the hearts of the fathers to the children, and the hearts of the children to their fathers, lest I come and strike the earth with a curse" (Mal. 4:6 NKJV, parenthesis added).

If a parent and teenager grow distant from each other, the probability is the parent will have little spiritual impact, even if the parent teaches biblical truth and lives out that truth before the teenager. Teenagers tend to reject truth when it comes from someone with whom they have a cold relationship.

Here is good news that flies in the face of popular thinking: teenagers *want* genuine relationships with parents and with other significant adults. Parents who want to have warm relationships with their children throughout adolescence need to know the children likely want the same thing.

Broken Heart Connections

Teenagers not connected to the hearts of their parents begin a desperate attempt to meet their own needs. Their spiritual and emotional tank that should have been filled by parents is painful while empty.

To make the pain stop, they create plans for filling the tank themselves. Unfortunately, their attempts to fill that tank while separated from parents and from God will be foolish. "Folly [or foolishness] is bound up in the heart of a child" (Prov. 22:15 NIV).

A fourteen-year old girl might leave the house for school wearing a revealing outfit. Below the level of consciousness, she might be feeling: *I don't know what happened to my dad and me. We used to be so close. He would hold me and tell me I was beautiful inside and outside. Then he just seemed to get busier. When I started changing and growing up, he wasn't around much, and he stopped telling me he loves me. Sometimes I get so lonely, and other times I just need his hug. . . . But the girls say there is a way you can get the boys to hold you and tell you that you're pretty—and even say they love you. And now I will do whatever it takes to make that happen.*

Injuries to Heart Connections

The beliefs, values, and ethics of parents positively influence the majority of children and teenagers. Similarly, the majority want to spend positive time with their parents. But a smaller group of teenagers is a clear exception. They want neither the opinions nor the presence of their parents. What went wrong?

Some teenagers have been wounded by the anger and emotional outbursts of parents. Yelling, screaming, or sarcasm almost never lead to positive behavior changes in teenagers. They represent terrible discipline. All they accomplish is emotional injury. Parents unwilling to change these patterns need to accept the fact that they will have increasingly limited influence in the lives of their teenagers.

Other teenagers push parents away in order to protect themselves from more hurt. They have been abandoned emotionally by parents preoccupied with career, income, self-fulfillment, failing marriages, new romances, adult recreation, community involvement, or even church busyness.

Counselors call these teenagers disconnected, wounded, or kids with emotional tanks running on empty. Unless something changes quickly, they likely will reject the faith.

Teenagers also can injure heart connections. They can hurt parents by their rebellion and disrespect. They can cause searing pain by dashing parents' hopes and dreams. They can injure parents who longed to see children living in moral purity but now only see immorality.

With respect and humility, church leaders gently can ask parents questions such as these:

1. If your teenager is genuinely pushing away your convictions and values and genuinely does not want to be around you, might he or she be reacting to emotional neglect?

2. Is it possible your drive to provide your child with economic advantages has caused you to be physically absent and emotionally drained and distant?

3. Is it possible your stressful marriage, new romance, or adult friendships have left you with little time or energy for your children?

4. Are you aware that if your teenager is emotionally abandoned by you, he or she almost certainly will reject your faith, make terrible lifestyle choices, and drift even farther away from you as an adult?

5. To keep from losing your children, are you and your spouse willing to consider making life-altering changes related to absence from the home and reserving emotional warmth for them?

6. With Scripture as your guide and Christ as your strength, will you commit to doing whatever it takes to provide your children with the unconditional love, sense of significance, and emotional security they must have to prosper?

7. If there is the need, will you do whatever it takes to heal an injury your child may be carrying from you? Are you willing to take the first step by asking for forgiveness?

8. If there is the need, will you forgive your teenager for hurting or disappointing you? As with Jesus and the soldiers at the cross (Luke 23:34), are you willing to forgive even if you are not asked to and even if your teenager doesn't deserve it?

Inoculating or Restoring Heart Connections

Parents and teenagers who have strong heart connections can inoculate those relationships to make drifting apart unlikely. Parents and teenagers who already have started drifting apart can restore the relationship they have lost.

The book *30 Days: Turning the Hearts of Parents and Teenagers Toward Each Other* (www.LifeWay.com) guides families through a powerful experience that builds or restores heart connections. Each evening a parent and teenager go to a room with a closed door and pull chairs near each other. They break the seal on the *30 Days* envelope for that night. For the first time they see the five cards for that evening. By following the instructions on the cards, the parent and teenager say and do those things that have the most powerful potential to turn their hearts toward each other.

Also, each evening they find a fresh way to pray together. Thousands of families have seen dramatic changes in relationships through this experience.

Words of Encouragement and Affirmation

Teenagers tend to embrace the faith of parents who communicate their significance, provide encouragement, and daily say, "I love you." Even during adolescence the most powerful words teenagers ever hear come from their parents.

- "Death and life are in the power of the tongue" (Prov. 18:21).

- "Do not let any unwholesome talk come out of your mouths, but only what is helpful for building others up according to their needs" (Eph. 4:29 NIV).

Sadly, some Christian parents communicate that they never are completely satisfied with what their teenager does. Their teenager may have come to believe he or she can never please the parent. The teenager could be pushing away the parent's faith only because the teenager finally gave up trying to please the parent.

Parents honor Christ by recognizing His worth is beyond any price. Similarly, parents honor children by considering them to be special gifts He has entrusted to them. Parents need to remind children *daily* how valuable they are. "Love each other with genuine affection, and take delight in honoring each other" (Rom. 12:10 NLT).

Focused Time with Teenagers

Children and teenagers tend to embrace the faith of parents who spend focused time with them. Here is a declaration two parents might make that flies right in the face of the so-called "American dream."

> We sometimes are frustrated with our modest house and neighborhood. If both of us stretched ourselves to the limit, we can see a way we could get into that better neighborhood. But while children are in our home, we are choosing something better. We would rather have a modest home filled with laughter, long talks, and relaxed evenings. We would rather see our children begin each day with their spiritual and emotional tanks brimming full. We would rather have time to gather at the end of the day to pray and speak of the things of Christ. We know there are better neighborhoods out there, but today we want something far better.

Teenagers don't embrace the supremacy of Christ because they go to better schools, wear the proper labels, or have more elaborate vacations. They become spiritually vibrant young adults because, in part, they spend powerful hours enjoying parents' focused attention. Christ is calling families to balance the time one or both parents spend working outside the home to rear a generation for His purposes.

Extracurricular activities should build emotionally and spiritually vibrant teenagers. When extracurricular activities take so much time they make time with parents and family impossible, then they no longer are accomplishing their purpose. Just because being on one team is good does not mean being on three teams is better.

If parents tend to push children to overextend in activities, they may need to ask some hard questions:

- Am I pushing my child to overextend in hopes he will excel because I need to prop up my weak self-concept by living vicariously through the successes of the child?

- Am I pushing my child to overextend in hopes she will win a major scholarship and thus allow me to hold on to college savings?

Here are the critical questions for parents:

- Has a family's schedule become so crazy that too few minutes are available for focused attention on children, quiet conversations, and even spiritual instruction and leadership?

- If the answer is yes, will a parent take a ruthless inventory to discover what is pulling family members apart evenings and weekends?

- Once a parent discovers what is causing the craziness in schedules, will the parent ask for God's leadership in knowing what changes must be made?

Warm, Intimate Marriages

Teenagers tend to embrace the faith of parents in a warm, lifetime marriage. Children and teenagers tend to embrace the faith of parents who surround them with emotional security. Believing the marriage of parents will last is a primary source of that emotional security. Questioning whether the marriage will last robs children of that security. That is one of many reasons God hates divorce (Mal. 2:16).

In this instance it does not matter whether parents think their marriage will make it. The children come to their own conclusions. When they hear muffled shouts coming from the master bedroom, or they detect icy stares between parents at dinner, or they see touching and flirting become rare, they make their own evaluation about whether the marriage will make it. If teenagers decide the marriage is not well, their emotional security vaporizes, and their behavior becomes consistent with insecurity.

Parents who have been wounded by a spouse may no longer feel motivation to rebuild romance from the perspective of his or her own needs. But kingdom parents find the motivation to rebuild what has been lost for the glory of Christ and for the good of their children.

When parents are warm and appropriately affectionate toward their spouse in front of the teenager, they are taking a giant step toward rearing offspring who will embrace the supremacy of Christ.

Parents Investing in Other Teenagers

As parents embrace the supremacy of Christ, they increasingly can make an eternal impact in the lives of teenagers from other homes. You can present these challenges to parents:

- You can share the good news of Christ with children and teenagers who do not yet know Him. You might say your home feels like Grand Central Station with children coming and going. Watch for conversations that can turn toward Christ.

- You can ensure teenagers who do not yet know Christ are welcomed and valued when the youth group gathers at your church. You can speak truth to parents who would push such students away.

- You can assist with supervision when the youth group gathers to ensure that including students who do not yet know Christ does not change the personality of the group.

- You informally can share truth with young believers who come under your roof.

- You can allow the Christian atmosphere of your home to make a lifetime impression on those who never see such a model. You can become intentional about letting others observe truth lived out in home relationships.

- You can help fill the emotional emptiness of children and teenagers who receive little love, affirmation, or focused attention in their own homes.

- You can become a prayer warrior for the teenagers who come to your home, in some cases becoming the *only* person who is bringing a child's name before Christ.

- In short, you can see your home as a primary mission field and an expression of your personal call to ministry.

Releasing Teenagers for Christ's Purposes

Student ministers and church leaders can look forward to a day when many parents will experience

an awaking to the supremacy of Jesus,
    and more deeply adoring Him on His throne,
        and daily arise to join Him in His kingdom activity.

Such parents will be able to look into the eyes of their children and say:

I declare you belong to Christ the King.

If you and I both come to believe Christ is calling you
to do something that involves risk, I will teach you
all I know about how to live wisely and safely. At the same time,
I will do nothing to stand in your way of following Christ's call,
no matter what the risk.

I hereby release you from any pressure to follow
in my vocational footsteps.
I charge you to do only what Christ calls you to do.

I acknowledge Christ may call you to a vocation that does not bring
financial wealth or worldly prestige. The great pride I will feel as a
parent will come from watching you do what Christ has called *you*
to do.

Someday you might be confronted by wicked people.
They may only give you two options—curse God or die.
I release you to honor God, even if it should cost you your life.

God often has used students to bring an awakening
to Christ in the church.
I pray God will honor our family by allowing you to be part
of such a generation.

I now consecrate myself to both teach and live before you
to prepare you for Christ's callings on your life.

Blessed be the name of the Lord.

One chapter is hardly adequate to cover the comprehensive subject of Christian parenting. Parents wanting to explore the subject further are invited to read *Parenting with Kingdom Purpose* by Richard Ross and Ken Hemphill. For more information about the book go to www.kingdomparent.com.

Student ministers can place in the hands of every parent an inexpensive but powerful resource called *Parenting Teens: Essentials for the Journey* by Richard Ross and David Booth. For full information, go to www. D6Family.com.

Chapter Thirteen
The Full Congregation and Prayer Mentors

Members of the congregation may not drive vans full of teenagers or help serve pizzas, but they help shape the effectiveness of your church's student ministry. They may be three or four times the ages of the teenagers, but they can be important to them.

Some adults are troubled by some of the trends and developments in the community, the nation, and the world. This chapter is built on the truth that it is better to light a candle than curse the darkness. Adults joining Christ in the life of a teenager provide a positive, hopeful way to create a more positive future. Some blessings adults will get to see with their own eyes, and some will emerge as a legacy from their lives for those who follow.

Today adults may or may not feel connected to the teenagers of your church. Adults may or may not sense teenagers want a relationship with them. You may or may not believe building bridges between adults and teenagers has been a priority for your church in the past. But the past is past, and it is time to move forward. The following background can make moving forward more purposeful.

The Genesis of Youth Culture

1. In the beginning, there were children and adults.

2. Around 1900, cultural shifts in American education, industrialization, and the law led to a new stage of life—youth.

3. At first youth were a high priority to parents and culture. The majority had their most basic needs met in stable families.

4. During the social upheaval of the late 1960s, a critical mass of Americans began to reject a relationship with God and obedience to His Word. America quickly moved toward becoming a post-Christian nation.

5. Since people always must have a god, many Americans replaced the God of the Bible with the trinitarian gods of personal happiness, personal peace, and prosperity.

6. Turning from God to a god or gods always has consequences. "And just as they did not see fit to acknowledge God any longer, God gave them over to a depraved mind, to do those things which are not proper" (Rom. 1:28). Adults became self-absorbed, incapable of lasting relationships, and generally living on the edge of chaos and breakdown.

7. What was once a relatively healthy adult community that highly valued the young became filled with many chaotic adults seeking their own survival.

8. On a national level this led many of the structures of society to abandon youth.

9. On a family level parents just trying to survive lost focus on the most basic emotional and spiritual needs of their children.

10. Abandonment became the most pervasive characteristic of teenagers.

11. Teenagers need adults as they struggle to become adults, and when adults were not present and involved in their lives, they were forced to figure out how to survive life on their own.

12. To survive, teenagers banded together to construct for themselves a matrix, an alternate reality to the adult world. Their matrix is composed of rules, value systems, and

norms; and to the teenagers who live in it, it is completely real.

13. Without the wisdom of adulthood, teenagers constructed a matrix (youth culture) that is dark, foreboding, and, as in *Lord of the Flies*, deadly.

14. Peer relationships form the core of the matrix. Teenagers know those relationships are transitory, often shallow, and even potentially dangerous. But in the absence of connections with key adults, they tenaciously hold to those relationships for survival. That is youth culture.

(If you wish to study more deeply the abandonment of America's teenagers, read Chap Clark, *Hurt: Inside the World of Today's Teenagers*, Baker Books, 2004).

The Church Mimicked the Culture

Churches watched the development of a youth culture in America. Even though the genesis of that youth culture was dysfunctional, the churches decided it would make a dandy pattern for ministry in the church. While teenagers banded together with little adult contact in the culture, the church created youth groups that would function much the same way.

Mimicking parents, many churches gave youth buses, buildings, and budgets instead of the relationships they longed for. Other churches gave neither resources nor relationships.

Today teenagers go along and support church youth programs as long as there is a momentary payoff, such as fun trips, glitzy youth centers, and more time with peers. As teenagers begin to approach graduation, these momentary payoffs become less important, and they disappear from the church.

They leave because they have experienced church mostly in teenage-only appendages and have not felt connected with the congregation. They leave, in part, because they have failed to build heart connections with their own parents or with significant adults.

What Can Be Done?

1. To move from surviving to thriving, teenagers need heart connections with both parents. They also need integrity relationships with a minimum of three godly adults outside the home.

2. Every spiritually and emotionally healthy adult of the church is a candidate for building integrity relationships with teenagers.

3. When Christian adults and parents passionately make teenagers a priority, meet their most basic emotional and relational needs, and then teach and model truth, then Christ, His Word, and His mission become more real to teenagers than the matrix.

4. Building designs, calendars, and programming elements must increasingly cause teenagers to feel connected with the full congregation.

5. Teenagers experiencing spiritual transformation in intimate community with adults as well as peers have the capacity to lead the church into an awakening to all Christ is today—if the Father should so lead.

6. Teenagers anchored to the significant adults in their lives have the passion and tenacity to rescue many of their peers from the matrix.

7. Teenagers increasingly allowing Christ to live His life through them—while living in vibrant relationships—have the courage and zeal to complete the Great Commission while they are young.

8. Teenagers who are valued, loved, and connected with godly adults and parents have the capacity to live or even die for no other motive than the glory of God.

Your Church as a Family for Teenagers

Scripture often refers to the body of Christ as a family (Gal. 6:10; Heb. 2:11). Teenagers often do not feel a part of the broad church family but perhaps stand in greatest need of the warm, family-type relationships it could provide.

Teenagers need to be immersed in a church family because many live with broken relationships with their biological families. Some parents, siblings, and extended family members are missing or estranged due to a divorce. Other family members may be physically present but toxic in relationships.

Churches that embrace teenagers into relationships can fill voids left by absent or unhealthy family members. Caring adults also can join the Great Physician in bringing healing to those who already have been wounded by life.

Often, extended family members may live too far away to provide the warmth and guidance teenagers need. That is a distinct by-product of this highly mobile society.

Church families can fill the gap by building around each teenager a web of relationships. For example, senior adults in the church can stand in the gap for students separated geographically from grandparents. They can provide the warmth, wisdom, and unfailing love every teenager needs.

You can decide that you will take steps to make your church a more welcoming family to teenagers. You can invite and challenge all ages of adults:

- To make positive comments about teenagers in groups, classes, and in services. Their positive thoughts will tend to be contagious with other adults.

- To support proposals under consideration that would communicate to teenagers that they are valued.

- To allow their face and body language to be welcoming when teenagers are nearby.

- To search out teenagers who have made a contribution during worship and affirm their gifts and desire to serve.

- To search out and affirm teenagers who have made public promises of moral purity or taken some other stand for their faith.

- To make a financial contribution to a youth unable to afford a church activity, adding a promise of prayers.

- To arrive on the parking lot in time to pray over and encourage teenagers about to leave on a mission trip or project.

Prayer Mentors

Even though some adults may desire to see impact in the lives of teenagers, they may sense they have not been called to disciple this age group or to serve as a typical student ministry volunteer. At the same time, they may gladly accept your call to invest in the life of one special teenager. They might express this call by becoming a prayer mentor.

Prayer mentors pray daily over a teenager, and they provide encouragement
and warmth to that student.
They reflect the heart of an older Paul toward Timothy,
"I constantly remember you in my prayers night and day,
longing to see you, . . . so that I may be filled with joy" (2 Tim. 1:3–4).

As student minister, you are called to equip the saints for the work of the ministry. You are called to equip volunteers and disciplers for the work of their ministries. You are called to equip parents for the work of their ministries. And you are called to equip adults to pray daily, deeply, and tenaciously over every one of your teenagers. The prayer mentor initiative opens the door to that third equipping ministry.

- Imagine adults lining up to have their pictures taken because they want their adopted student to know who has made a commitment to pray for them every day until they graduate from college or get married.

- Imagine a pipeline of Christ's power and protection flowing into your students' lives every day through prayer.

- Imagine more adults praying the second year than the first and more the third year than the second.

- Imagine your students receiving regular notes of encouragement from the people who care enough to pray for them every day.

- Imagine students who are stronger and steadier in their faith because they feel the prayers and support of their prayer mentors.

- Imagine having a prayer mentor you quickly can e-mail any time you learn of a crisis affecting that mentor's student.

- Imagine having a host of prayer mentors you quickly can e-mail anytime the overall student ministry is facing a great challenge or opportunity.

- Imagine seeing a young man carrying a gift-wrapped box at church and discovering it's his birthday and the gift is from his prayer mentor.

- Imagine knowing adults are praying for a young generation to lead the church in an awakening to God's Son.

Bottom line: God blesses prayer and the nurturing connection formed between two generations.

Look forward to the day when prayer mentors might:

- Show the most delight when a teenager walks into the auditorium.

- Guarantee a teenager will receive at least one hug while at church.

- Affirm the gifts and abilities they see in a teenager.

- Express genuine interest in a teenager's future education, vocation, and family.

- Build up a teenager in conversations with the parents.

- Celebrate a teenager's making a clear promise of moral purity or taking any other public stand for King Jesus.

Many teenagers today are missing relationships that could be valuable to them. Prayer mentors can be part of the solution. They can:

- Introduce their teenagers to their extended family.

- Introduce their teenagers to other members of the congregation who can bless teenagers' lives.

- Introduce their teenagers to adults who can help open doors related to education, present employment, and future vocation.

Relationships are powerful, but prayer is the heart of prayer mentor relationships. Those prayers can flow in both directions. Teenagers who develop heart connections with their mentors may well begin to pray for their mentors. Adults can discover power in prayer as a teenager brings the mentor's name before the throne every morning. Over time that may well mean prayer requests begin to flow both directions.

The Shout Prayer Mentor Initiative

See You at the Pole was ignited by one church in Burleson, Texas. True Love Waits emerged from one church in Hermitage, Tennessee. In the same way Steve Gervasi's vision—leading to praying adults in a church in Columbia, Tennessee—has launched a nationwide prayer initiative.

Those at the heart of the Shout Prayer Mentor Initiative are in the trenches in local-church student ministry, live exemplary lives, and believe deeply in prayer. They live in financial simplicity to free resources for the multiplication of prayer over students. They are trustworthy partners for student ministers ready to mobilize scores of adults to pray over students.

The Shout Prayer Mentor Initiative is built on three commitments:

1. For an adult prayer mentor to pray for his or her assigned student every day.

2. For the prayer mentor to continue to pray for his or her assigned student until he or she graduates from college or is married.

3. For the prayer mentor to encourage his or her student several times a year with notes that communicate, "I'm still here and I'm still praying for you."

Keys to Effectiveness

Scores of churches that have embraced the prayer mentor initiative have discovered:

1. The senior pastor's excitement about and commitment to the initiative and the three commitments (noted above) are most important to a successful ministry.

2. The student minister's passionate concern for having every student covered in daily prayer is the second most important ingredient.

3. A gifted, motivated prayer mentor initiative coordinator is the third most important factor.

4. A well-crafted communication/promotion plan is the fourth most important key.

The PMI Coordinator

Coordinating the Shout PMI requires more time than most student ministers have available. Wise student ministers call out and equip a leader to serve as a coordinator for this ministry. This person:

1. Must have a heart for seeing every student covered with daily prayer.

2. Must know how to be a team player.

3. Must have basic computer skills.

Support

The Exchange Network supports the Shout Prayer Mentor Initiative with:

- The comprehensive Web site www.shoutpmi.org, where student ministers should go first to learn more about the initiative.

- Extensive administrative materials.

- Video/audio (or on-site) training.

- Print and media support for Shout Sunday (which typically leads to mobilizing 25–40 percent of the adults on Sunday morning to pray for students).

- A Web page for each student, giving mentors an understanding of their student and giving students a place to post prayer needs.

- A Web dashboard that allows the student minister and the PMI coordinator to see all that is happening with students and mentors.

- E-newsletters to mentors that provide insight into the world of teenagers, motivation, and deepening instruction in prayer.

- Postcards mentors can send to their students.

Closing

Pray for a day when adults in your congregation will pray:

Exalted Christ,
introduce me to the teenager You have chosen for me.
For the glory of Your Father and in the power of Your Spirit,
let me see that teenager
increasingly embrace Your full supremacy,
responding to Your majesty in all of life, and
joining You in making disciples among all peoples.
To that end,
awaken me to more of who You are today.
Prepare me to adore Your dazzling radiance.
And glorify Yourself as I arise to join You in the life of this teenager.

Chapter Fourteen
After High School

Students are most likely to embrace the full supremacy of Christ for a lifetime when they have heart connections with significant adults in their lives who increasingly embrace the full supremacy of Christ. That is the bottom line. No warm and intimate relationships with parents, disciplers, and the congregation? No adults around who are vibrant and alive with new discoveries about Immanuel? Then college mission trips and dorm Bible studies are less likely than keg parties, one-night hookups, and Sunday morning snoozing.

Losing 50 to 70 percent of faithful church youth after high school graduation is a crisis. Most leaders now are aware of the situation. Many voices are suggesting solutions. Some of those solutions will help a little and should be implemented. But the bottom line remains. Until churches begin to experience an awakening to much more of who Christ is today and until leaders immerse teenagers in relationships with awakened adults, then the number of students walking off the cliff after high school will not change much.

Overlap the Gap

Student ministry professor Wes Black notes there is always a gap between train platforms and the steps of the train. If a traveler is preoccupied, he easily can step into that gap and thereby break a leg or twist an ankle. Knowing this, the conductors standing on train platforms in Europe always shout, "Mind the gap. Mind the gap."

Likewise, students face a gap between high school and college. Students have been falling into this gap and hurting themselves and others. But another gap is sitting right on top of the gap between school experiences. Just when students are most vulnerable, most churches have created a gaping gap between high school ministry and collegiate ministry. Just when high school graduates stand at a crossroads, youth workers are waving good-bye, dusting their hands, and deleting students' records from their computers. At that same moment collegiate ministers only know these teenagers as new names in their database.

How did the church decide that placing one gap right on top of the other was the best plan? It is time to overlap the gap.

A *relationship* with God through Christ as presented in Scripture is the heart of the Christian faith. A *relationship* also is the conduit or pipeline that primarily carries biblical truth and spiritual impact to the heart of a student. Consequently, *relationships* must be at the heart of overlapping the gap. The five adults who most invested in a student during his or her senior year are the key.

Parents—Parents tend to stay in relationship with their son or daughter after high school. The church's eighteen-year investment in their family will help determine whether that relationship is warm and rich or cold and distant. But even the most spiritually alive and emotionally healthy parents will need guidance in learning to parent a young adult living away from home. Many otherwise wonderful parents do not know how to make this transition. Churches that gather parents to address this issue provide valuable service. Parents who navigate the transition well are in the best position to allow their own awakening to Christ to permeate the lives of their children living away.

Disciplers—When enlisting a discipler, you might say, "If Christ should so lead, we are inviting you to enter a discipling relationship with three students that might extend one year past high school graduation. Even if some or all of your students move away, we are inviting you to continue investing in their lives through calls, online communication, and time together when they are home."

Disciplers probably won't try to move through a formal curriculum while students are away, but they still can share biblical truth and engage students in careful thinking about their faith. Disciplers can be trained to give special support at critical times, such as the first days of school and prior to spring break.

Prayer Mentors—Prayer mentors bring to the table both prayer and relationships. Both can go right on past high school. As with disciplers, prayer mentors should be enlisted with a view toward the relationship extending past graduation. In fact, if students and older adults truly have bonded during high school days, they are going to want to stay in contact with or without an official plan. Older adults increasingly are comfortable online. Many will find ways to stay connected to students living away and ways to learn how they can pray more specifically.

Student Ministers—After sharing life for six or seven years, most student ministers have a special bond with recent high school graduates. That bond can be a valuable source of inspiration and guidance after graduation. The key is for student ministers to view them as part of their flocks for a year past high school. Staying connected and providing touches of ministry then will come naturally.

Student ministers might lead their churches to add an item to their job descriptions: "Accept primary responsibility for guiding the church's relational ministry to and with students for one year after high school graduation." Note the word *relational.* This clarifies that the student minister guides the church to address relational issues and not program issues with these students. The collegiate (or young adult) ministries of a church provide Bible studies, worship, mission trips, and other programming elements for students just out of high school. The student minister (i.e., the minister to middle and high school students) typically does not provide programming for those a year out of high school but does stay connected in relationships.

In order for their student to participate in a senior recognition Sunday near graduation, families might be invited to commit:

1. To attend the senior recognition breakfast/luncheon as a family and complete the information requested there.

2. To attend the senior recognition breakfast/luncheon and worship service one year later.

Students and families returning a year later gives high visibility to continuing ministry provided by the student minister, parents, volunteers, and the congregation. Students with uninvolved parents who will not attend senior recognition Sunday might attend senior Sunday events with their discipler, both after graduation and one year later.

At a senior recognition breakfast/luncheon, graduates and families can be invited to turn in:

1. The college/trade school/military base the student will attend, lodging location, cell phone number, and online addresses.

2. The date of the first day the student will be on campus.

One year later returning students can be invited to share at the breakfast/luncheon or during the worship service how Christ has been active in their lives. All year they can know this opportunity is coming.

Soon after senior recognition Sunday, the student minister might meet with the pastor and the leader of the church's collegiate/young adult ministry. This meeting represents the passing of a baton as the student minister transfers to the collegiate minister primary responsibility for relational ministry for those one year past high school. The student minister might turn in a portfolio which includes:

1. The spiritual status and church/ministry relationships of each student who participated in senior recognition Sunday one year previous.

2. A report on ways the summer was used to prepare students to leave home and enter college/trade school/military life.

3. A report on ways the summer was used to prepare parents to be spiritual leaders and provide support for their college/trade school/military sons and daughters.

4. A report showing each student had contact information for at least one church and one campus ministry the day he or she arrived at college.

5. A report showing information about each student was sent to at least one church and one campus ministry before the student arrived on campus.

6. A report showing ways the student minister stayed connected and provided touches of ministry during the year.

7. A report showing ways disciplers, prayer mentors, current youth group members, and the congregation were mobilized to stay in contact with those who left for college/trade school/military.

Many Christian organizations are networking to assist students and churches in addressing the issue of the transition from high school to college. You will find wonderful partners in ministry at www.youthtransitionnetwork.org. Wes Black has provided seminal research on the issue with his Faith Journey of Young Adults study. You can see the research and the implications for student ministry at www.sltn.com/FJYA/Study/intro.htm.

You probably are working so many hours a week that your health and family are at risk. Expanding your flock and responsibilities without some adjustments may not be reasonable. This may be a time for your church to consider:

- Adding a paid intern or associate.
- Removing an existing responsibility from your job description.
- Adopting lead teams to guide major events.

A GAP Year Mission Trip Following High School

Students who joyfully are awakened to their King Regent begin to adore Him more passionately. But the exuberance of adoration is not the end. Students who have seen Jesus high and lifted up tend to shout, "Send me!" They know arising to join Him in bringing His kingdom on earth will be the greatest adventure of their lives. Increasingly, students awakened to Christ will be open to going to the front lines of kingdom expansion while they still are young. Envision it becoming normative in your church that almost every student serve full-time in domestic or international missions for a summer, semester, or year, around age eighteen or nineteen.

Working in concert with established missions and missionaries, students on such missions adventures could take the good news of Christ in their lifetime to the last groups of people on earth both in the U.S. and around the globe. They could have a part in planting indigenous churches that disciple believers and continue to carry the good news of Christ in their cultural context.

Every Christian student should go on short-term mission projects throughout adolescence and beyond. But at least once every student needs the life-altering and kingdom-expanding challenge of going to the front lines for a longer period. Every church youth group should do mission projects together. But at least once, *all* students need to go without the group to do what God uniquely has called and gifted them to do.

Developmentally, eighteen- and nineteen-year-olds crave a grand adventure. They are ready to do the hard thing and go to the hard places. This is the perfect time for an assignment so challenging it requires all they are and all the Spirit supplies.

Though students need leaders to guide them in strategy, they can be effective in sharing Christ. They tend to share their faith without fear. In almost every region of the world, youth are fascinated with American students and are motivated to talk with them. Even adults find youth far less intimidating than adults who share their faith. The proliferation of students on missions adventures in the U.S. and worldwide could result in immediate increases in people coming to know Christ.

Society increasingly is using the term *GAP year* to refer to a student who takes time from university studies for an extended trip or some immersive experience. Increasingly, universities are granting admission to high school graduates but not requiring them to register for classes for one year. That period might easily become an extended missions adventure. Those who name this adventure a GAP Mission Trip can understand GAP to mean **G**o **A**nd **P**roclaim.

Envision parents opening savings accounts at the birth of babies that eventually will fund GAP mission trips. (Envision that for now, parents of all ages of children and youth open accounts.) Currently, students can sell candy in the church lobby or write support letters to fund their ten-day mission trip. Such plans are inadequate for raising the $6,000–$25,000 that might be needed for longer missions adventures. Family savings seem to be the only viable plan.

Parents who open a missions savings account at the birth of a child will have no problem saving what is needed over a period of eighteen years. And they may be pleasantly surprised at the number of relatives and friends who want to ensure that savings are adequate. Grandfather might say to the family gathered at Christmas: "You know we are going to sell this big house to move into something more manageable. We think there might be some funds left over when we do. For all you children with missions savings accounts, we want to add $1,000 to each so we can be a part of what you do for the kingdom someday."

Wise pastors can present a small check to parents during family/baby dedication. He might say, "We, your church family, want to be the first to contribute to your son/daughter's future missions adventure. We invite you to go to your bank tomorrow and use this check to open a savings account for that purpose. Then, as Christ leads, we invite you to contribute monthly to that account for the next eighteen years or so. Other relatives and believers likely will make contributions as well. Then, when the Spirit tells your son/daughter it is time to go, funding will be in place for this grand adventure."

The funding of students to do full-time missions should measurably increase giving to existing missions offerings. When a church becoming more alive to Christ sends its own members to do direct missions, both their special missions offerings and their regular offerings tend to go up.

Parents who experience the thrill of their own children serving alongside missions organizations will always have more interest in the financial support of those ministries. Also, the students who have seen God at work in North American and international missions always will have a bond with those movements. Those bonds can lead to missions giving for a lifetime.

Envision churches filled with eighteen- and nineteen-year-olds arising to join their King. Church attendance among high school seniors falls precipitously during the final months before graduation. Preparation for a missions adventure soon after high school could become an exciting, energizing focus for one's senior year at church.

Leaders could introduce the year by asking new seniors: "Are you fully prepared to share Christ in a clear way with any person you meet?" "Do you feel competent to answer many of the tough questions people may have about the Bible?" "Are you so consistent in your morning worship and Bible study that your quiet time sustains you during lonely or difficult days?" Seniors recognizing they need much training before going out to a challenging assignment may remain active through graduation and beyond.

Similarly, students returning from serving Christ all day every day for months may well become vibrant members and leaders in their college churches. It is difficult to imagine hardly any dropping out. If missions adventures were to become normative, perhaps this would help mark the end of the mass exodus from church after high school.

- Picture a day when most grade schoolers in your church will look forward to a GAP mission trip after they finish high school.

- Picture a day when one of the most common decisions at student conferences will be students confirming their time to go has arrived.

- Picture a day when parents whose hearts have been softened by saving funds for eighteen years will *celebrate* hearing their son or daughter knows it is now time to go, even if the trip will involve risk.

- Picture a day when your church collegiate group and local campus ministry will be infused with the passion of Christ from students constantly returning from their mission adventures.

Envision a day when most of the adults in the church have as part of their heritage a season when they joined King Jesus on the front lines of kingdom advancement.

- Would it change the spiritual climate of your church if almost all adults who teach the Bible had as part of their life story a time they went to the front lines of missions?

- Would it change the quality of decisions made by your church if almost every deacon/elder/leader in your church had spent months in 24–7 kingdom activity?

- Would the spiritual impact of parents on children be any different if those parents had spent a GAP year completely immersed in Christ's ministry?

It is time for the church to make it normative that almost every student serve full-time in domestic or international missions for a summer, semester, or year, around age eighteen or nineteen.

Appendix A
To the Pastor

Your time is valuable, and you do not have time to read anything not vital to your life and ministry. You may wisely decide to skip several chapters in this book. But chapters 3, 4, and 5 are not the chapters to skip. What you are about to read will make little sense without the perspective presented in those chapters. Reading them before returning to this appendix represents your best use of time.

Your awaking to the supremacy of Jesus, your more deeply adoring Him on His throne, and your inviting Him to live His life through you offers the best hope for your congregation moving in those same directions.

Your highest priority, both personally and vocationally, is to journey toward deeper love and worship of the Father, more fully embracing the full supremacy of His Son, increasingly becoming conformed by the Spirit to Christ's image, and joining Him in making disciples among all peoples.

Embracing that priority will change things.

- It will shape your hope for the future.

- It will shape the content of your prayers.

- It will shape your worship before the throne.

- It will shape your attention to the spiritual disciplines.

- It will shape the books you read and the people with whom you pursue a relationship.

- It will shape your meditation on the Scriptures that present the supremacy of God's Son.

You will need to take specific steps to implement a new paradigm of student ministry. But nothing you *do* will ever be as important as who you *are*. If you experience an awakening to more of who Christ is today, this change in you may spread throughout the congregation. The beginning point is your deciding to pursue a journey of discovery into more of who Christ the King is today.

Your View of Student Ministry for the Future

Now that you have read at least chapters 3–5, you have decisions to make before you can lead your church to make changes.

Do you desire:

- To see teenagers awakened to the supremacy of the Son of God?

- To see teenagers adore Christ as they discover and embrace more of who He truly is?

- To see teenagers inviting Christ to live His life through them?

- To see teenagers and the full church experience an awakening to Christ for all He is today?

- To see teenagers deeply devoted to Christ and His church into adulthood?

Do you believe these outcomes are more likely:

- When parents awakened to the supremacy of Christ serve as the primary spiritual leaders to their own children?

- When you and the student minister live out before teenagers your own awakening to the Son of God?

- When volunteers awakened to the supremacy of Christ disciple teenagers in integrity relationships?

- When members of the congregation awakened to the supremacy of Christ envelope teenagers in warm and caring relationships?

- When teenagers awakened to the supremacy of Christ live in biblical community with their peers?

- When the student minister partners with you and other leaders to lead adults who are significant to students increasingly to embrace the supremacy of Christ?

- When the student minister guides planning teams in designing programming that brings together students and the significant adults in their lives?

- When teams of students, parents, and volunteers make most preparations for major events and ministries so the student minister can shift time to higher priorities?

If you happen to believe most of these are true statements, then you will be valuable as you guide your congregation in considering change in the very DNA of student ministry.

Your Leadership

- Your preaching and teaching about concerted prayer will be important for calling out believers who will immerse this entire process in prayer.

- Your preaching and teaching about the primacy of parents as spiritual leaders can change their sense of call.

- Your preaching and teaching about the potential students have for the kingdom can alter how the congregation views them.

- Your preaching and teaching about Christ's love for the church can lead students to value the congregation.

- Your preaching and teaching that speaks positively about students and avoids speaking critically about students (even in jest) can change impressions about them.

- Your preaching and teaching that calls every believer to have a ministry can lead adults to commit to discipling students or serving as their prayer mentor.

- Your preaching and teaching about discipling can lead believers to want to disciple or to be discipled.

The most common question leaders will ask as they read this book will be, "Where on earth are we going to find that many adults who will become involved with teenagers?" That question often will be followed by, "How do we find enough adults when over half the teenagers in our church attend without parents?" And, "We can't fill the leadership positions with students now. How on earth would we double that number?" Such sincere questions deserve sincere consideration.

Here is a fact:

> **Churches where most adults continue to see Christ**
> **more as a mascot than a Monarch**
> **will find it impossible to implement fully**
> **the new paradigm of student ministry**
> **described in this book.**

Someone has said, "If you keep doing what you have been doing, you will keep getting what you have been getting." If spiritually plateaued adults have not responded to calls to service in the past, they probably won't today. Telling them they *ought to,* or telling them louder, or making them feel guilty will not motivate them for long.

On the other hand, if adults begin to be *awakened* to much more of who God's Son is today . . .

- That usually leads to their *adoring* Him with much more depth and exuberance.

- That usually leads to their *arising* to join Him in entirely new kingdom activity.

- That might well include their fresh commitment to impact the lives of teenagers.

No other approach to mobilizing the church holds much promise.

Evaluation

You will need to ensure the church is clear about how the student minister will be evaluated in the days ahead. Otherwise, the student minister will be at risk during days of such deep change in student ministry. Some voices may call for ministry to students to remain unchanged. Other voices may call for changes to be implemented even faster. Some voices may affirm that the student minister is leading the church in valuable directions. Other voices may say the changes are damaging.

In this new paradigm student ministers need a job description that has been updated to reflect changes in the church's new approach to student ministry. If one group in the congregation wants the student minister to spend more time entertaining students and another group applauds time spent investing more in volunteers and parents, an irresolvable situation may result. An approved job description becomes the clear guidance needed to approach student ministry.

Student ministers deserve to know officially whether they are performing well. They need to know what criteria are used in making that decision. Vocational student ministers need to know how their work will be evaluated and how such evaluations might affect salary decisions. They need to know how to respond to negative feedback from church members when that feedback is at odds with the official evaluations of church leaders.

Forty Days toward Change

Ideally, all the stakeholders in student ministry need to link arms to pray, study, and discuss the possibility of making major shifts in the church's ministry with students and families. Then, as they sense Christ's leadership, they need to make those changes together.

Leading many vocational ministers, volunteers, parents, and leaders in the congregation to read this book may dramatically accelerate change. Your reading the book alone is like lighting a little kindling next to logs soaked in water. Your getting many to read the book is like lighting a little kindling next to logs soaked with kerosene.

You and the student minister can consider linking arms to lead the church through forty days toward change. Forty days is not enough time to *implement change*. It is enough time to *decide to change*. If leaders pray, seek leadership from God's Spirit, and consider what He whispers in their ears, then the church can change much of its thinking about student ministry in forty days. Appendix E contains details of such a forty-day process.

Students under your ministry during their teenage years are much more likely to spend a lifetime embracing the full supremacy of the Son, thinking and acting as He does, and joining Him in making disciples among all peoples if your church experiences an awakening to the King of glory. Your life and your preaching and teaching may be the key to that awakening. Like nervous grade-school boys standing on a high cliff over the lake, someone must jump in first. That person is you.

Appendix B
Daily Devotionals

Below is a suggested format for spending some personal time with the Lord Jesus each day. This format offers one possibility, but you may think of even better approaches. The daily themes can help you gain "the light of the knowledge of the glory of God in the face of Christ" (2 Cor. 4:6 NIV).

May your experience with the King over the coming month cause you to see His face in whole new perspectives, to know Him more fully for all He is, to awake to the fullness of His supremacy, to adore Him increasingly as your King, and to arise gladly to join Him in the acceleration of His kingdom purposes.

Daily Format

1. Read (one or both passages).
2. Awake (use some or all of these study questions).
   A. What is the most important insight you gain from this passage about the supreme majesty of God's Son?
   B. Why is this dimension of His supreme majesty so important for you to know and believe?
   C. How might this facet of Christ's kingship be seen somewhere in the world today, in the acceleration of His kingdom purposes?
   D. How might this dimension of Christ's reign make a difference in what you share with someone today, in your ministry today, or in a decision or task you face today?
   E. How can you join God in awakening others to this dimension of His Son's majesty?

3. Adore (praise and worship the King).
4. Arise (possible applications to your life).
5. Journal (journal your thoughts).
6. Listen (be silent before your King).

WEEK ONE: Who He Is *to* Us

Sunday: His supreme majesty flows from His eternal relationship to the Father as the Son.
    John 17:1–5, 24–26
    Psalm 2:4-12

Monday: His supreme majesty flows from His very nature and character as God's holy Son.
    John 1:1–4
    Isaiah 11:1–10

Tuesday: His supreme majesty is manifested in His creation of all things.
    Colossians 1:15–17
    Proverbs 8:27–36

Wednesday: His supreme majesty was displayed when He became one of us to live among us.
    Luke 2:25–31
    Isaiah 9:1–7

Thursday: His supreme majesty was magnified as He died for our sin, defeating sin, bearing God's judgment.
    Colossians 1:18–19
    Isaiah 53:4–12

Friday: His supreme majesty was vindicated when He rose again, conquering death for us forever.
    1 Corinthians 15:20–28
    Psalm 16:5–11

Saturday: His supreme majesty was sealed when He ascended to heaven to be crowned King of kings.
Hebrews 7:24–26
Psalm 110:1–7

WEEK TWO: Who He Is *over* Us

Sunday: His supreme majesty is exercised as Ruler of history.
Revelation 5:4–10
Daniel 7:9–10, 13–14

Monday: His supreme majesty is exercised as Lord of the nations.
Philippians 2:8–13
Haggai 2:6–9, 20–23

Tuesday: His supreme majesty is exercised as Head of the church.
Ephesians 1:18–22
Psalm 72:1–14

Wednesday: His supreme majesty is exercised as Master of your life and mine.
Romans 14:4, 8–9
Micah 5:2–5

Thursday: His supreme majesty is demonstrated as He leads us forth in His triumphal mission.
2 Corinthians 2:12–16
Zechariah 9:9–17

Friday: His supreme majesty is demonstrated as He goes ahead of us to defeat our enemies.
Revelation 3:7–10
Micah 4:1–8

Saturday: His supreme majesty is demonstrated whenever He opens for us new doors of opportunity to serve Him.

    Matthew 16:16–19, 24–25, 28

    Isaiah 40:1–11

WEEK THREE: Who He Is *within* Us

Sunday: He reigns supreme in us and among us as He empowers us to be pure and holy.

    John 15:4–8, 16

    Malachi 3:1–4; 4:1–3

Monday: He reigns supreme in us and among us as He reproduces His risen life within us.

    Philippians 1:9–11, 20–21

    Ezekiel 37:22–28

Tuesday: He reigns supreme as He pulls His people together around Himself in true unity.

    Ephesians 2:13–18

    Zechariah 12:7–13:3

Wednesday: He reigns supreme through us as His Spirit fills us to share His love with others.

    Ephesians 14:14–21

    Isaiah 61:1–4

Thursday: He reigns supreme by how He uses us to advance His kingdom among those near to us.

    Acts 1:3–11

    Isaiah 42:1–4

Friday: He reigns supreme when He transforms communities and campuses through us as we share the fruits of His reign where we live.

    Acts 11:20–26

    Amos 9:11–15

Saturday: He reigns supreme by how He uses us to advance the kingdom among the unreached peoples in our nation and in other nations.
Romans 15:15–21
Isaiah 60:1–7

WEEK FOUR: Who He Is *upon* Us

Sunday: His supreme majesty increases whenever we *seek* more of His reign in our lives.
Philippians 3:7–14
Psalm 21:1–8

Monday: His supreme majesty intensifies as God's Spirit *awakes* us to more of what His reign should mean in our lives.
Matthew 11:25–30
Jeremiah 33:3, 10–17

Tuesday: His supreme majesty is magnified as God's Spirit helps us *adore* more of His reign in our lives.
Revelation 1:12–18
Isaiah 52:7–15

Wednesday: His supreme majesty accelerates as we *arise* boldly to join His reign everywhere.
Acts 4:24–33
Joel 2:28–33

Thursday: His supreme majesty enlarges our hope about His return in kingly glory.
Titus 2:11–14
Zechariah 14:1–9

Friday: His supreme majesty ignites our passion to see Him take charge of the rest of eternity.
2 Timothy 4:1–2, 6–8
Isaiah 55:1–3

Saturday: His supreme majesty will dominate our desires and our praises as we worship and serve Him as our King forever.

Revelation 22:1–5, 12–17

Zephaniah 3:8–20

Appendix C
Student Minister Job Description

This is a sample job description. The language and format need to be customized to a particular situation.

The student minister, for the glory of the Father and in the power of the Spirit, increasingly embraces the full supremacy of the Son, responds to His majesty in all of life, invites Christ to live His life through him, and joins Him in making disciples among all peoples.

The student minister guides believers to join Christ in ministry that leads to students who do the same for a lifetime.

The Student Minister Will:

Minister

- Serve as an integral member of the pastoral ministry team.
- Give full support to the leadership role of the senior pastor.
- Provide pastoral ministry with students and their parents and leaders.
- Coordinate the training of others to do likewise.

Administer

- Coordinate student ministry organizations and ministries.
- In cooperation with church leaders, coordinate an overall curriculum plan, leading to properly sequenced, balanced, and comprehensive discipleship for students.

- Coordinate the creation of the annual student ministry budget proposal, and administer that budget according to church policies and procedures.

- Coordinate space utilization in student ministry and make recommendations concerning building and remodeling needs.

- Coordinate the training and mentoring of students sensing a call to ministry vocations.

- Coordinate planning to ensure students and their parents are directly involved in missions and ministry, both locally and away.

- Coordinate planning to ensure Christian students experience authentic worship personally, with the student group, and with the full church body.

- Coordinate planning to ensure students experience true fellowship within the student group and the full body of Christ.

- Accept primary responsibility for guiding the church's relational ministry to and with students for one year after high school graduation.

Lead

- Guide spiritually sensitive students, parents, and volunteers to define and communicate the church's student ministry purpose and strategy.

- Partner with preaching and teaching leaders, in the power of the Spirit, to lead significant adults in the lives of students to embrace the majesty of Christ.

- Partner with preaching and teaching leaders, in the power of the Spirit, to lead significant adults in the lives of students to build heart connections with those students.

- Partner with preaching and teaching leaders, in the power of the Spirit, to lead parents of students to be effective, biblical parents and spiritual leaders in their homes.
- Chair the core planning team and annually lead it in prayer-filled, strategic planning.
- Guide the core planning team in designing programming that allows students and the significant adults in their lives to live out the supremacy of Christ together.
- Guide the core planning team in designing programming that allows students to build heart connections with peers.
- Guide the core planning team in designing programming that allows students to embrace and live out the supremacy of Christ with peers.
- Represent student ministry during churchwide strategic planning.
- Coordinate student ministry lead teams.
- Coordinate the enlisting, discipling, training, and motivating of volunteers to serve in student ministry, in concert with church policies and procedures.
- Coordinate the permeating of student ministry with prayer.
- Fine-tune skills in leading, administering, ministering, and communicating through a structured reading plan, high-quality conferences, and formal education.

Communicate
- Preach and teach biblical truth.
- Share the gospel on an ongoing basis with lost students and lost parents of students, both individually and corporately.
- Coordinate an overall strategy for evangelizing lost students and lost parents of students, including frequent training for students in personal evangelism.

- Equip students, parents, and volunteers to understand student culture, to make biblical decisions about involvement with the culture, and to become agents of change in the culture.

- Network with other student ministry leaders in the community to support students in starting and strengthening school campus ministries and to coordinate events designed to evangelize and disciple students.

- Coordinate the training of students to serve as missionaries to their homes, schools, communities, and world.

- As allowed by law, represent Christ on secondary school campuses within the sphere of influence of the church.

- Coordinate student ministry communication and promotion plans in concert with lead teams, student organizations, and church leaders.

Accountability

- The student minister reports to the _____ and supervises _____.

Appendix D
True Love Waits

The Web site www.truelovewaits.com presents a comprehensive view of the international True Love Waits movement. The site also presents about everything youth leaders and parents need to know to carry the movement to their own communities and families. The site always has links to the freshest resources for carrying the challenge of purity to teenagers. To all that is available on the Web site, I want to add several first-person reflections.

The Origin of the Idea

As True Love Waits started to explode in 1993, my wife said to me, "You know, the Lord Jesus loves His kids way too much to let them be sucked under by the culture. We are watching His strong arm pull these teenagers away from harm and toward His heart. It is so clear to me that Christ and Christ alone is orchestrating everything about True Love Waits." As usual, my wife's insights were right on target.

Jimmy Hester and I sketched out True Love Waits on napkins during break times in the LifeWay cafeteria. But it would be the height of arrogance for us to pretend those ideas came from our intellect. In a sense we were just taking dictation. Christ just as easily could have led two youth leaders in Fargo, North Dakota, or Addis Ababa, Ethiopia, to take down His ideas. Jimmy and I have enjoyed a grand adventure with True Love Waits, but we never forget who started and who sustains this precious movement.

The Big Picture

New student ministers who never have seen the full message of True Love Waits might assume it is "this deal where you sign some card or something, and then you try real hard not to have sex until marriage."

Like salvation, True Love Waits is a process. The Holy Spirit orchestrates many messages and influences for the person He is leading toward salvation. Then, in His timing, redemption occurs at a point in time. Then Triune God leads the church to come alongside that new believer and leads him or her toward transformation.

Similarly, True Love Waits includes all the family and the church do to prepare a teenager for a clear promise of purity. And True Love Waits includes the moment that promise is made. And True Love Waits includes all the family and church does to equip and encourage the teenager to live out all the implications of that promise.

A Focus Every Year

Almost every Sunday morning I'm in a different pastor's office. Often the ministers gather for prayer before I preach that morning. Before we pray, here is what they often say: "Oh, Richard, we are just thrilled with what God has done through True Love Waits. What a powerful movement that literally has brought positive change to the U.S. and now to the world." (So far so good, but then comes the following.) "In fact, we so believe in True Love Waits that we provided a beautiful promise ceremony here three years ago."

Though I keep a smile on my face, thoughts whirl through my mind. A service three years ago? Teenagers who entered puberty at eleven or twelve have reached ninth grade with no opportunity publicly to proclaim their promise of purity? Seventh graders now fascinated with oral sex go all year with no invitation to promise purity to God? Eighth graders who go to parties where the girls give the boys "rainbows" (don't ask) go yet another year with no promise? High school juniors who gloriously meet Christ graduate with no opportunity to stand tall for purity in a worship celebration? Families with teenagers join the church but then wait three years before they are challenged to slip a promise ring on their teens' fingers?

TRUE LOVE WAITS®
A LifeWay Ministry

The Call of God

Grace & Forgiveness

Example & Instruction from Parents

Example & Instruction from the Church

Example & Encouragement from TLW Teenagers

The Promise

Made to Almighty God

Confirmed by a Signature

Remembered with a Concrete Symbol

Made in the Presence of Parents

Made with the Blessing of the Church

The Power of God

Warmth & Encouragement from Parents

Structure & Supervision from Parents

Encouragement & Accountability in the Church

Unity & Accountability with TLW Teenagers

Today a generation...
- confused about what sex is
- confused about their gender
- abused by their elders
- diseased and dying
- parenting too early

Tomorrow a generation...
- living for the glory of God with sails raised for revival
- prepared for biblical, lifetime marriages
- persistently pure in thought, look and touch
- emotionally and spiritually vibrant and alive

Perhaps church leaders shy away from an annual promise ceremony because they don't want to ask a student to make six promises while young. They have missed the point. We never ask teenagers to make multiple promises. In fact, it offends Christian students when they are asked to promise again. In their minds their original promise was a promise to God, and that promise stands to their wedding day and beyond.

The annual invitation to participate in a promise ceremony is made only:

1. To middle schoolers just promoting into the student ministry.

2. To students who have made commitments of their lives to Christ in the previous year.

3. To students who have joined the church and have no background with True Love Waits.

Students who have made promises in previous years participate in Bible teaching on purity, and they attend the ceremony to support the first-timers, but no one places yet another card in their hands.

During the next Valentine season, tens of thousands of churches will provide beautiful, moving services and ceremonies built around promises of purity. Some churches won't. When churches go more than a year without inviting their teenagers to settle this issue before God, they are placing those kids at risk. Maybe someone should place this on the agenda for the next church staff meeting.

A Cause for Concern

Preceding the rise of True Love Waits there were twenty unbroken years of increase in teenage sexual activity. Consequently, teen pregnancies, abortions, births, and sexually transmitted diseases all rose precipitously those years.

On April 21, 1993 the fifty-three original TLW teenagers from my youth group shared about their promises with a thousand student ministers meeting in Nashville. Upon hearing what these young people had done, the student ministers jumped to their feet and clapped, cheered, and wept for almost ten minutes. Everyone in the auditorium knew God was launching something far beyond what we could imagine. The next day those student ministers returned to their home states and lit the fires for a movement. Almost overnight leaders and parents in multiplied thousands of communities were preparing students to make promises of purity.

The rising graph of teenage sexual activity plateaued and then turned down. As a result, teen pregnancies, abortions, births, and sexually transmitted diseases have fallen since that time . . . until now. Just before this book went to press, this report appeared:

> More teenagers and young adults are having sex, sparking an increase in teen births in both 2006 and 2007, and putting an end to more than a decade of significant decline. . . .
>
> To make matters work, sexually transmitted diseases (STDs) among young Americans are also on the rise. . . . The troubling news comes from the Centers for Disease Control and Prevention (CDC) in their Morbidity and Mortality Weekly Report. The researchers concluded from their findings, ". . . Earlier progress appears to be slowing and perhaps reversing."[1]

In 1994, youth leaders, parents, and core students leaned hard into the movement for purity. The statistics fell, untold human tragedies were prevented, and great glory ascended to the God of purity. By 2009 many youth leaders had moved away from an annual focus on purity promises. The statistics started moving up again. This generation of student ministers will determine what the future will bring.

Criticism

Some student ministers have been confused by magazine articles that seem to indicate True Love Waits "doesn't work." Some background can be helpful.

Research in recent days has found a disappointing number of students who made some type of abstinence pledge and then later became sexually involved. But these studies lump together *all* students who have made *any* type of pledge or promise. This includes those who sign a page in their notebook after one or two health class presentations on disease and pregnancy. None of us should be too surprised that some students who make superficial "promises," especially at school, later become sexually involved.

Right now we are waiting on funding for a national research project that exclusively will study whether True Love Waits students tend to keep their promises. Then we will be able to prove to the watching world that a promise to God is far more powerful than a promise to a notebook, that a promise made surrounded by one's family and church is more powerful than one made in a classroom, and that Christian students who link arms to stand for purity together tend to live lives different from those who struggle alone.

But for now it is interesting to note the vociferous opposition by many in government and academia to the issue of abstinence. Some are finally beginning to say out loud what their agenda may have been all along. Some honestly believe sexual expression should be a joyful part of teenage living and that cautioning teens about early sex is impinging on their "rights." Focus on the Family reports:

> A flurry of news stories proclaiming abstinence education does not decrease unwanted pregnancies among unmarried teens, and that teaching it is dangerous, prompted one group to investigate the source of those claims.
>
> The Medical Institute for Sexual Health—a nonprofit organization dedicated to evaluating scientific evidence—examined two recent reports in the *Journal of Adolescent Health*. The position papers, written by a team headed by John Santelli, maintained that abstinence education is "scientifically and ethically problematic." The authors claimed that teaching young people to postpone sexual activity until marriage is "inconsistent with commonly accepted notions of human rights."

In a news story on July 15, 2009, Lifesitenews.com reported from England that "Steve Slack, Director of the Centre for HIV & Sexual Health at National Health Service Sheffield, told media that as long as teens are fully informed about sex and are making their decisions freely as part of a 'caring relationship,' they have as much right as an adult to sex."[2]

At the time this book was written, government funding for abstinence education was being cut dramatically. In the public square, church leaders and parents have every right to weigh in on this issue, knowing all children and youth who attend school deserve to know the advantages of waiting on sex until marriage.

But for believing families, it never was the government's role to teach sexual values to their children. Maybe an era of reduced focus on abstinence in the schools will cause parents to step up to the plate and do what Christ has commissioned them to do. Maybe student ministers now will view an annual focus on purity as central to achieving their mission.

The goal of all student ministry is young believers who, for the glory of the Father and in the power of the Spirit, spend a lifetime embracing the full supremacy of the Son and responding to His majesty in all of life. Sexual purity is a powerful way to acknowledge the supremacy of Christ. It permits students to stand before the throne and adore and worship Him without guilt or shame. And sexual purity allows students to move out in kingdom activity with great passion and power. Avoiding STDs and not having early babies are good things, but they pale in comparison with our focus on bringing great glory to Christ through a generation who abides in Him in purity.

Appendix E
Forty Days toward Change

Many books can help a church fine-tune its student ministry. This book probably is not one of them. This book advocates radical change simultaneously impacting students, parents, volunteers, and the full congregation. Piecemeal change is not going to work too well.

The naval armada of student ministry in your church needs to turn all at one time, or ships are going to start crashing into one another. Ideally, all the stakeholders in student ministry need to link arms to pray, study, and discuss the possibility of making major shifts in the church's ministry with students and families. Then, as they sense Christ's leadership, they need to make those changes together.

The senior pastor must take a major leadership role for such far-reaching changes to be possible. He must be convinced that present ministry models are not adequate and that a new paradigm is essential. Then he and the student minister can link arms to lead the church through forty days toward change.

The Goal of the Forty Days

Forty days is not enough time to *implement change*. It is enough time to *decide to change*.

If leaders pray, seek leadership from God's Spirit, and then implement what He whispers in their ears, then the church can change much of its thinking about student ministry in forty days.

- Forty days is not enough time to pair all students with prayer mentors, but it is enough time to open teenage and adult hearts to such relationships.

- It is not enough time to enlist and train sufficient adults to disciple students, but it is enough time to convince many this relationship can be powerful.

- It is not enough time to get every family worshipping at home, but it is enough time to lead most parents to believe they are to be the most important spiritual leader to their own children.

- It is not enough time to organize lead teams for every major event coming in the future, but it is enough time to convince most that this plan offers many advantages.

Practical Matters

Note that the first large gathering of students, volunteers, and parents occurs during a Bible-teaching hour on Sunday morning. For churches that have such an hour, this time period offers the best opportunity for gathering the largest number of those three audiences. Sadly, parents and students on the fringe of church life usually will not attend such a gathering any other time.

If the information shared in this first gathering captures the hearts of those present, it is then possible they will return for all the noon meetings and other gatherings. Getting their ear first during the Bible-teaching hour makes it well worth the administrative hassles of releasing them from their regular study groups this one time.

Churches that have multiple Bible-teaching hours on Sunday morning can ask families to adjust their schedules to attend the same hour this one time, or the presentation can be repeated during each of the sessions. Churches that have only worship on Sunday mornings can use a noon luncheon for the initial gathering.

To relieve budget pressures, consider charging for noon meals. Remind parents their meals are costing less than if they went out to eat. Following the meal, provide child care for younger children so parents can focus on presentations.

Day One: Wednesday

Preview the Forty Days

- Assemble core students, volunteers, and parents.
- Preview with them the issues making up the forty-day focus.
- Answer their questions and prepare them to be early advocates with others.
- Provide time for concerted prayer.

Day Three: Friday

Pray into the Night

- Assemble praying students and adults to pray all night or into the night.
- Adore the Son of God in worship and praise.
- Invite the Father to exalt His Son before your church.
- Ask for wisdom in setting new directions for the church.
- Ask the Holy Spirit to open the hearts of adults and students to those new directions.
- Pray for a full awakening to all Christ is today.

Day Five: Sunday

Sunday Morning Sermon: *Who Is Christ: Mascot or Monarch?*

Student Minister's Testimony in Morning Worship: *The Crisis in Student Ministry*

- Students graduating from high school also are "graduating from God."
- Replacing parents with church leaders has not worked.

- Segregating students from the congregation has not worked.
- It is time for change.

Day Twelve: Sunday

Sunday Morning Sermon: *The Son from Eternity Past*

Student Minister's Testimony in Morning Worship: We are focusing our student ministry on the supremacy of God's Son and the power of relationships between students and significant adults.

Bible Study Hour: Assemble all students, volunteers, and parents. Build a Case for Change
- The goal of student ministry is students who embrace the supremacy of Christ all of their lives.
- Students are most likely to embrace the supremacy of Christ when the significant adults in their lives do.
- Students who experience heart connections with the significant adults in their lives are most likely to reflect those adults' awakening to Christ.

Day Nineteen: Sunday

Sunday Morning Sermon: *The Son's Incarnation, Death, and Resurrection*

Noon Luncheon: Assemble all students, volunteers, and parents. Present a new paradigm of student ministry that:
- Recognizes parents as the primary spiritual leaders of students.
- Immerses students in relationships with at least five godly adults.

- Provides programming that supports and trains parents and volunteers and deepens heart connections between students and those adults.

Day Twenty-Six: Sunday

Sunday Morning Sermon: *The Son's Coronation and Reign Today*

Student Testimony in Morning Worship
- We want and need you to disciple us and reveal to us the majesty of Christ.

- We grow fastest while sharing life with someone in relationship.

- This offers you a way to leave a legacy of your life.

Noon Luncheon: Assemble all students, volunteers, and parents. Present the lead team strategy.

Student Testimony in Student Bible Study or Student Worship: Friends are valuable, but we also need to share life with a discipler who can guide us to embrace the Son of God.

Day Thirty-Three: Sunday

Sunday Morning Sermon: *The Son's Return and Eternal Kingdom*

Student Testimony in Morning Worship: We want and need you to be prayer mentors with us.

Older Adult Testimony in Student Bible Study or Student Worship: My generation desires a relationship with you and will be blessed by your passion for Christ. You may be separated from your grandparents, but we stand ready to love you, encourage you, and pray for you.

Day Forty: Sunday

Sunday Morning Sermon: *Christ the King of our Hearts, Families, and Church*

Family Testimony in Morning Worship: We desire our home to be the place where parents and children awake to more of who Christ is, adore Him with all our hearts, and arise to join Him in great kingdom adventures.

Noon Luncheon: Assemble all students, volunteers, and parents.
- Use skits to demonstrate family worship.
- Present a resource to use in family worship.
- Allow families to experience family worship.

Appendix F
Exemplary Youth Ministry Study
and This Book

The purpose of the 2005 Exemplary Youth Ministry Study was to identify congregations that consistently establish faith as a vital factor in the lives of their youth, to discover what accounts for their effective approach to ministry, and to make the results widely known for the benefit of other churches.

Churches of all sizes from seven denominations participated in the three-year study. These churches, located in all parts of the United States, represent what many consider the most effective youth ministries today. Six thousand youth and adults completed extensive questionnaires (265–354 items) about all aspects of a church's youth ministry. Then twenty-one exemplary congregations were selected for in-depth on-site visits. Research teams interviewed youth, youth leaders, parents, youth ministers, other staff, and pastors. The result is a unique combination of statistical and interview data in a massive data bank which helps to guide and shape youth ministry.

Listed below are the forty-four characteristics that congregations with exemplary youth ministry tend to share. Beside each characteristic are the page numbers which allow the reader to see how that quality is captured by the youth ministry model in *Student Ministry and the Supremacy of Christ*.

Congregational Assets

Theological Character

1. God's Living Presence—Possesses a sense of God's living presence in community, at worship, through study, and in service. Pages 12, 32

2. Centrality of Faith—Recognizes and participates in God's sustaining and transforming life and work. Pages 13–19

3. Emphasizes Prayer—Practices the presence of God as individuals and community through prayer and worship. Pages 63–70

4. Focus on Discipleship—Committed to know and following Jesus Christ. Pages 89–112

5. Emphasizes Scripture—Values the authority of Scripture in its life and mission. Pages 91–92

6. Centrality of Mission—Consistently witnesses, serves and promotes moral responsibility, and seeks justice. Pages 75–88

Pastoral Leadership

7. Spiritual Influence—Knows and models the transforming presence of God in life and ministry. Pages 197, 200

8. Interpersonal Competence—Builds a sense of community and relates well with adults and youth. Pages 199–200

9. Supports Youth Ministry—Understands, guides, and advocates for youth ministry. Page 200

10. Supports Leaders—Affirms and mentors youth and adults leading youth ministry. Page 199

Congregational Qualities

11. Supports Youth Ministry—Youth and ministry with young people are high priorities. Pages 176–83

12. Demonstrates Hospitality—Values and welcomes all people, especially youth. Page 178

13. Strives for Excellence—Sets high standards, evaluates, and engages in continuous improvement. Page 53

14. Encourages Thinking—Welcomes questions and reflection on faith and life. Pages 94–95

15. Creates Community—Reflects high quality personal and group relationships. Page 131

16. Encourages Support Groups—Engages members in study, conversation, and prayer about faith in daily life. Pages 92–99

17. Promotes Worship—Expands and renews Spirit–filled, uplifting worship through the congregation's life. Pages 70–72

18. Fosters Ethical Responsibility—Encourages individual and social moral responsibility. Pages 73–74

19. Promotes Service—Sponsors outreach, service projects, and cultural immersions both locally and globally. Pages 78–83

20. Demonstrates Effective Practices—Engages in a wide variety of ministry practices and activities. Pages 75–88

Youth Involvement

21. Participate in the Congregation—Youth are engaged in a wide spectrum of congregational relationships and practices. Pages 37,134

22. Assume Ministry Leadership—Youth are invited, equipped, and affirmed for leadership in congregational activities. Pages 135–37

Youth Ministry Assets

Youth Minister

23. Provides Competent Leadership—Reflects superior theological, theoretical, and practical knowledge and skill in leadership. Pages 209–10

24. Models Faith—Is a role model reflecting a living faith for youth and adults. Pages 113–15

25. Mentors Faith Life—Assists adult leaders and youth in their faith life both one–on–one and in groups. Page 117

26. Develops Teams—Reflects clear vision and attracts gifted youth and adults into leadership. Pages 49–58

27. Knows Youth—Knows youth and changes in youth culture and uses these understandings in ministry. Pages 131–32

28. Establishes Effective Relationships—Enjoys effective relationships with youth, parents, volunteers, and staff. Pages 121–27, 131–32

Youth and Adult Leaders

29. Equip for Peer Ministry—Youth practice friendship, caregiving, and outreach supported by training and caring adults. Pages 104–5, 135

30. Establish Adult–Youth Mentoring—Adults engage youth in faith and life supported by informed leadership. Pages 92–99

31. Participate in Training—Evaluate and equip youth and adults for ministry in an atmosphere of high expectations. Pages 53, 105–7

32. Possess Vibrant Faith—Youth and adult leaders possess and practice a vital and informed faith. Pages 125–26

33. Competent Adult Volunteers—Foster authentic relationships and effective practices with youth within a

clear vision strengthened by training and support. Pages 39–44

Youth Ministry Effectiveness

34. Establishes a Caring Environment—Provides multiple nurturing relationships and activities resulting in a welcoming atmosphere of respect, growth, and belonging. Page 39

35. Develops Quality Relationships—Develops authentic relationships among youth and adults establishing an environment of presence and life engagement. Pages 132–34

36. Focus on Jesus Christ—The life and ministry of Jesus inspires the ministry's mission, practices, and relationships. Pages 31–32

37. Considers Life Issues—The full range of young people's lives is valued and addressed. Pages 95, 101, 111

38. Uses Many Approaches—Intentionally, creatively employs multiple activities appropriate to the ministry's mission and context. Pages 53–54

39. Organized Well—Engages participants and leaders in long–range planning, implementation, evaluation, and innovation in an atmosphere of high expectations. Pages 49–62

Family Involvement

40. Possesses Strong Parental Faith—Parents possess and practice a vital and informed faith. Pages 146–150, 159–61

41. Promotes Family Faith Practices—Parents engage youth and family in conversations, prayer, Bible reading, and service that nurture faith and life. Pages 149–50, 154–56

42. Reflects Family Harmony—Expressions of respect and love create an atmosphere promoting faith. Pages 63–70

43. Equips Parents—Offers instruction and guidance that nurture parental faith and equip parents for nurturing faith at home. Pages 159–61

44. Fosters Parent–Youth Relationships—Offers parent-youth activities that strengthen parent–youth relationships. Pages 160–61

For full information about the exemplary youth ministry study, go to www.exemplarym.com. Registering on the site provides full access to all study background and reports.

Endnotes

Chapter 2

1. Rick Lawrence, *Jesus-Centered Youth Ministry* (Loveland, CO: Group Publishing, 2007), 33, 46.

2. Christian Smith with Melinda Lundquist Denton, *Soul Searching: The Religious and Spiritual Lives of American Teenagers* (New York: Oxford University Press, 2005), 162–63.

Chapter 3

1. David Bryant, *Christ Is All* (New Providence, NJ: New Providence Publishers, 2005), 16.

2. Dietrich Bonhoeffer, *Ethics* (New York: Touchstone Press, 1995), 61 in ibid., 198.

Chapter 4

1. Jonathan Edwards, *Thoughts on the Revival of Religion in New England* (New York: American Tract Society, 1845), 410, in Jonathan Edwards, *The Works of Jonathan Edwards*, 1:423.

Chapter 5

1. David Kinnaman, *Most Twentysomethings Put Christianity on the Shelf Following Spiritually Active Teen Years* (September 11, 2006), www.barna.org, accessed July 28, 2009.

2. Leonard Sweet and Frank Viola, *A Magna Carta for Restoring the Supremacy of Jesus Christ* (http://ajesusmanifesto.wordpress.com, accessed June 29, 2009).

3. Merton P. Strommen and Richard A. Hardel, *Passing on the Faith: A Radical New Model for Youth and Family Ministry* (Winona, MN: Saint Mary's Press, 2000), 176.

Chapter 6

1. Doug Fields, *Purpose-Driven Youth Ministry* (Grand Rapids, MI: Zondervan, 1998), 60–65.

2. Ibid., 66–68.

3. Ibid., 87–90.

4. Sweet and Viola, *Magna Carta.*

Chapter 7

1. Rick Lawrence, *Jesus-Centered Youth Ministry* (Loveland, CO: Group Publishing, 2007), 44.

Chapter 8

1. Kevin Kirkland, *Broken Walls and Those Who Repair Them* (Longwood, FL: Xulon Press, 2009), 127.

2. Jack Hayford and Dick Eastman, *31 Days Meditating on the Majesty of Jesus* (Carol Stream, IL: Tyndale House Publishers, 2007), 152.

3. Greg Stier, *Outbreak: Creating a Contagious Youth Ministry through Viral Evangelism* (Chicago: Moody Press, 2003), 21.

4. Ron Hutchcraft, *The Battle for a Generation* (Chicago: Moody Press, 1996), 182–83.

5. Francis Chan, *Crazy Love* (Colorado Springs: David C. Cook Publishers, 2008), 117.

6. Ibid., 95.

7. Alex and Brett Harris, *Do Hard Things* (Colorado Springs: Multnomah Books, 2008), 25.

8. J. Hudson Taylor, *China's Spiritual Need and Claims*, http://en.wikiquote.org/wiki/James_Hudson_Taylor, accessed July 29, 2009.

9. Erwin McManus, *An Unstoppable Force* (Loveland, CO: Group Publishers, 2001).

10. Billy Graham, "Let Us Light a Fire," *Decision Magazine* (October 2000).

Chapter 9

1. Barry Shafer, *Unleashing God's Word in Youth Ministry* (Grand Rapids, MI: Zondervan, 2008), 45–46.

2. J. Scott Duvall and J. Daniel Hays, *Grasping God's Word* (Grand Rapids, MI: Zondervan, 2005), 20.

3. Shafer, *Unleashing God's Word*, 75.

4. Greg Ogden, *Transforming Discipleship* (Downers Grove, IL: InterVarsity Press, 2003), 54.

Chapter 10

1. Mark DeVries in Rick Lawrence, ed., *Jesus-Centered Youth Ministry* (Loveland, CO: Group Publishers, 2007), 145.

Chapter 12

1. Smith and Denton, *Soul Searching*, 56.

2. Strommen and Hardel, *Passing on the Faith*, 85.

3. Ibid., 179.

4. Josh McDowell, "It's Almost Too Late," *New Man Magazine,* June 2003, 56.

Appendix D

1. Healthnews.com, accessed July 24, 2009.

2. Lifesitenews.com, accessed July 28, 2009.